Elaine Lewis was born in Victo  the country town of Heyfield. In 1956 she graduated from the University of Melbourne with a Mus.Bac. (piano & singing).

After her marriage, she lived and taught for many years in Hamilton, Victoria. Returning to Melbourne she wrote musical courses for Distance Education.

From 1984 to 1995 she lived in Sydney, where she continued writing educational material and published *Let's Celebrate Music* – Books 1 and 2 with tapes (Dominie Publications). She also taught singing, piano and other music subjects, later studying Ethnomusicology at the University of New South Wales, where she gained her M.Mus. in 1991.

In 1996 she established the Australian Bookshop in Paris. She is currently involved in research, writing and translation.

Elaine's website is www.australianbookshop.com.au.

LEFT BANK WALTZ
THE AUSTRALIAN BOOKSHOP IN PARIS

Elaine Lewis

V
VINTAGE

A Vintage Book
Published by
Random House Australia Pty Ltd
20 Alfred Street, Milsons Point, NSW 2061
http://www.randomhouse.com.au

Sydney   New York   Toronto
London   Auckland   Johannesburg

National Library of Australia
Cataloguing-in-Publication Entry

Lewis, Elaine.
Left Bank waltz.

ISBN 1 74051 349 5.
ISBN 978 174051 349 4.

1. Lewis, Elaine. 2. Booksellers and bookselling – France –
Biography. I. Title

381. 45002092

Cover illustration courtesy Les Editions du Pacifique
Cover design by Christabella Designs
Australian Bookshop logo (L'Oiseau-Lyre) designed by Julie Scobeltzine
Typeset by Midland Typesetters, Australia
Printed and bound by Griffin Press, Netley, South Australia

10 9 8 7 6 5 4 3

CONTENTS

This book is for my children – David, Richard and Ginny; for my grandchildren – Ross, Harry, Grace, Niamh, Mia and Ella; and for all the wonderful people who helped me live the dream. Thank you.

Prelude

THE DREAM TRAVELLING-TRUNK

When I was eighteen I bought it from an elderly French-woman who lived in our small Victorian country town – a huge cabin trunk, covered in faded stickers with addresses from all over the world: Raffles Hotel, Singapore; Le Crillon, Paris . . . As high as a small wardrobe, it opens out flat to reveal drawers and a fold-out hat cupboard on one side and coathangers above shoe-storage bags on the other. The interior of the cabin trunk is upholstered in a rich, blue fabric and in it I store my personal souvenirs and lots of dreams. It is a reminder of the days of my youth, when people travelled to Europe by ship and I used to dream of one day standing on the deck of an ocean liner at Station Pier, Port Melbourne, waving goodbye and throwing streamers into the crowd, which would, of course, be singing 'Auld Lang Syne'.

Chapter 1

AN UNFORGETTABLE MOMENT

'There are two kinds of people in life: people who see the world as it is and wonder why. People who imagine the world as it should be and wonder: why not?'

'Dans la vie, il y a deux categories d'invidus: ceux qui regardent le monde tel qu'il est et se demandent pourquoi. Ceux qui imaginent le monde tel qu'il devrait être et se disent: pourquoi pas?'

George Bernard Shaw

PARIS, 1984

Swept along by the chattering crowd, David and I climb the exterior steps of the ornate Garnier Opera House at Place de l'Opéra in Paris. By daylight the nineteenth-century building is solid and imposing, but this evening, as we pass through the entrance hall and see the marble- and onyx-decorated staircase, surrounded by statues and glittering chandeliers, it seems like an extravagant fairyland. Everywhere I can see gold and red, nymphs and cherubs, velvet and gold leaf and myriad dancing colours in the spectrums glittering from the crystal prisms.

My son is a musician living in Paris. We are together here at the Paris Opera for an evening of ballet performed by the American Martha Graham Ballet Company, with Rudolph Nureyev as principal dancer. Nureyev was appointed Artistic Director of the Paris Opera Ballet twelve months ago and already his volatile personality has given rise to rumours that he will be leaving. This might be my only chance to see him live because next week I return to Australia.

⌀⌀ ⌀⌀

Here we are then, perched on gilt chairs with red velvet upholstery, sitting in a box, trying to ignore the crowd standing behind us and gazing at the enormous crystal chandelier illuminating the vivid colours of the Chagall ceiling – enclosed in two concentric circles are swirls of burnt sienna, dark moss-green and that unique French blue (is it *bleu de Lectour*?), all of them enhanced with faint smudges of purple. Mythological figures and angels, birds and well-known Parisian landmarks, all seem to float through the clouds, their more subtle colours contrasting with the solid reds and golds of the Opera House décor. It's very festive and adds to the atmosphere as we begin to feel more and more caught up in the excited anticipation of the audience.

Suddenly the music starts, the lights are dimmed and our attention focuses on the ballet. Tonight the audience is hushed and receptive – such is the power of the perform-ances. The dance seems to be about tension and release and this results in movements which at times look hard and angular but are, nevertheless, spectacularly beautiful.

The final piece of ballet on the programme is a new solo dance, choreographed by Martha Graham, the founder of this company, and performed by Nureyev. Dancing in bare feet, he moves with a fierce kind of energy and fluidity and such is his charisma that the whole audience seems capti-vated and involved.

At the end Nureyev acknowledges the wild, ecstatic applause and then, to the surprise of all, leaves the stage.

People are murmuring. Surely someone will explain? After what seems a very long wait, Nureyev reappears with Martha Graham herself on his arm.

Graham is over eighty years of age and has quite recently choreographed the dance we've just seen. The French Government has just awarded her the prestigious *Chevalier de la Légion d'Honneur*, an award created by Napoleon and given to either French citizens or foreigners for outstanding achievements in military or civil life. People leap to their feet with loud cheers of '*bravo*' and endless slow clapping, caught up in a kind of mutual ecstasy. It is the most exciting theatrical experience of my life.

Martha Graham, a small, captivating figure dressed in a sweeping black gown, is walking slowly and gracefully, with her head held high. She doesn't speak. There is no need because the emotional atmosphere she has helped to create conveys so much more than words could.

This is an unforgettable and inspirational moment that changes me instantly. Having experienced a rather acrimonious divorce, and now entering my fifties, I have lately been struck by a feeling that perhaps it is too late to chase dreams. This woman, almost twice my age and still actively participating in a creative life and giving so much of herself to others, is to me a sign that age doesn't matter. Without uttering a word, she seems to radiate energy and an enthusiasm for living that is contagious.

I become more determined than ever to change my life and extend my horizons. It isn't too late, after all, to combine my past experiences and passions to forge a new career – the possibilities are endless . . .

I leave the auditorium wrapped in dreams.

Chapter 2

SEDUCED BY PARIS AND JAZZ

'There is nothing like dream to create the future. Utopia to-day, flesh and blood tomorrow.'

Victor Hugo, *Les Misérables*

PARIS, 1984

It is winter in Paris and I am still overwhelmed by this city and the joy of being free to explore the stories behind the monuments, the buildings, the cafés and the streets themselves. And the people! I am fascinated with the language and can speak enough French to eavesdrop and try to understand a little of the conservations of people who inhabit *la ville de lumière* and I know that I want to come back, one day, to become part of it all.

Today is the eighteenth of January. My son, David, is studying trumpet at the Paris Conservatoire – his day is over and we are exploring the city by foot. He is a great walker and, with him, I have discovered the pleasures of strolling around what is really not a very large city. It is now late evening and we are in the Bastille area, which is a bit run-down and frequented mainly by writers, musicians, film-makers and other artists.

This *quartier* (neighbourhood), in the 11th *arrondissement* (district), has a laid-back, leisurely feel to it and rue de Lappe, with its dance halls, still evokes memories of the days of the *bals musettes*, during the nineteenth century when people came from all over Paris to dance in the cafés and bars first opened by the Auvergnats who settled here.

The Auvergnats had left the harshness of their mountainous Auvergne region in the Massif Central of south central France to search for a better way of life in Paris. They brought with them their traditional music and dance. In those days the dancing was often accompanied by the *musette*, a kind of bagpipe, and the piano accordion, of course. Italians, who later settled in the nearby 19th arrondissement, also contributed to the rise of the *bals musettes* and their popularity was such that, after World War I, the French upper classes began visiting these poorer quartiers, looking for excitement and entertainment.

We leave rue de Lappe and are meandering along rue du Faubourg Saint-Antoine when we become aware of music – above the rhythmic swing of drums a rich, flowing saxophone solo ends and a muted trumpet takes over with a spikier, more frenzied melody. It's exciting and enticing so we decide to follow the sounds, and soon we are descending a flight of well-worn stone steps into a mediaeval *cave*, or cellar, packed with people listening to music played by a jazz quintet who look as though they are having a great time. There's a pianist, a double bass player, a trumpeter (who also plays cornet and flugelhorn), a guitarist and a drummer, but from time to time friends from the audience are invited to join in, playing whatever instruments they have brought with them.

Their music is a kind of free jazz, with basic structures

that the instrumentalists improvise around as they wish, according to their abilities and tastes. All of the musicians are extraordinarily generous towards each other – there's no sense of competition as they concentrate appreciatively on the solos, getting caught up in the rhythms and improvisations and adding to the excitement by their responses to each other. It is this generosity of spirit, along with the exciting music, which permeates the atmosphere of the cellar with its stone walls and ancient oak beams. It's a glorified jam session, really, and we feel honoured to be part of it. The musicians seem to be a mix of African-French, European-French and the odd American, but judging by their conversation they are all Parisians.

The people in the audience, some sitting on the red velvet banquettes lining the edges of the room and others standing amidst clouds of smoke, are moving in time with the beat and listening intently. They seem to be a mixture of young and old, united in their appreciation of the music. This is one of the things I enjoy most about the jazz scene in Paris: it's not just the domain of the young.

Among the audience are some of David's musician friends and, in between sets, they wander over to say *bonjour* and chat about the music. I too enjoy participating in discussions about music so join in and am both amused and flattered when one young American musician turns to my son and says, 'Gee, Dave, your Mom's hip!'

I'm seduced by the atmosphere and say to my son, 'Wouldn't it be wonderful to create a space like this and play Australian music? Perhaps we could promote Australian wine and cheese as well?'

Having taught music at both secondary and tertiary levels and listened to a lot of Australian music, I've often thought that it would be wonderful for more of our great Australian musicians to become part of the international music scene. At present I'm thinking of jazz and I reflect that the two main jazz centres of the world still seem to be Paris and New York. Many jazz musicians pass through these two cities so they are the obvious places for significant cultural exchanges. Surely, I tell myself enthusiastically, it would be advantageous for more Australian musicians to travel and communicate with artists of the world. Who knows, perhaps these exchanges could even contribute to better international understanding.

Much later, back in my hotel room, I can't sleep for thinking about the logistics of such an enterprise. The thought of the expense of transporting Australian musicians and their instruments to Europe soon makes me realise that, as an entrepreneurial venture managed by one person, the reality of this idea could soon become a nightmare. But I don't give up – the idea is too alluring for that.

It's not long before my mind turns to books. I've always loved reading. When I was small it was wartime and there was a paper shortage so there were few children's books in our house. I read all the adult books on our bookshelves and my knowledge of other people's lives was gleaned from such books as *The Scarlet Pimpernel, Little Women, Pear's Encyclopaedia* and the works of the English Romantic poets – in particular Tennyson, Browning, Shelley and Keats. Later, when books became readily available, I read widely. More recently I've worked in bookshops and loved meeting people and selling books so, I think, why not live in Paris and create a small, independent bookshop, which could provide a space to promote all of the arts through books and other organised events? In a city where the word 'Australia' tends to evoke the response '*kangourou*' or '*oh, c'est loin*' (it's a long way away), it could promote Australian culture and be a meeting-place for artists of all kinds and for the general public in France.

With more than twenty years' experience of organising creative events and having loved teaching both children and adults, the idea of promoting Australian books in Paris excites me. I begin to think that, in some ways, running a bookshop with its associate activities would not be so very different from what I've done in the past.

At the end of my marriage I felt diminished and unable to make decisions. I had never really needed to think for myself before. Choices were made for me and I just went along with them. This holiday in Paris is the first time

I've travelled alone and I've been free to spend the whole five weeks with young people who have accepted me and involved me in their activities. Revitalised and inspired, I feel energetic and confident enough to follow through with my idea.

Thus a whole new world opens for me and the idea of creating a little bookshop in Paris seems entirely possible. Martha Graham and the evening in the jazz club have both somehow convinced me and the next day I return to Australia with my head in the clouds. I am determined to follow up the idea of creating an Australian bookshop in Paris. There is, indeed, life after fifty.

Chapter 3

THE BIG RED BOOK

'After all manner of professors have done their best for us, the place we are to get knowledge is in books. The true university of these days is a collection of books.'

Albert Camus

SYDNEY, 1984

Back in Sydney, I am sustained by the possibilities opened up for me by my short stay in Europe. An Australian bookshop in Paris! Until now I was satisfied with reading about Paris and dreaming of it in a general way, but now I have my own personal dreaming. To be honest, from the age of fourteen I have wanted to live within a different culture and, having been interested in France for more than forty years, Paris is the obvious choice.

Most Australians I know have a mythical image of Paris as a dream city and the image varies according to what they have read and experienced. Although we may complain from time to time about the actions of certain political leaders or of the complications of French bureaucracy, the fact is, if you mention perfume or fashion, gourmet cuisine, wine, cheese or, of course, romantic love, many Australians instantly think of France. Articles on France fill the lifestyle and travel sections of our magazines and newspapers. Though many of the articles are repetitive, it seems we can't get enough of people's adventures in Paris and other corners of France.

As a student I too fell in love with France – I sang French songs, played the music of Ravel and Debussy, memorised

French poetry, devoured as many French novels as I could find and began going to see French films. In the fifties, my friends and I considered ourselves rather daring, viewing foreign films in tiny theatres in the city, but the idea of actually living in Europe simply never occurred to most of us. In those days people were still travelling overseas on big ocean liners and to do this required both time and money, neither of which was available to students like me, tied down by teaching bursaries and other commitments.

So here I am, thirty-five years later, planning to turn a dream into reality. So far I have told only my three children – David, Richard and Ginny – that I want to create an Australian bookshop in Paris and they have been understanding and encouraging. They are all adults now and are independent and adventurous. I decide not to tell other people about my plan because I don't yet know when I can begin and I don't want them to smile knowingly and think it's just another pipe dream. But from the moment I return to Sydney I begin planning, determined one day to realise my aim. I know some people live for impossible dreams but I think I am too much of a realist for that. I think my dream is possible.

એ⊙ ⊙ગ

For the first time in my life I am planning ahead instead of just allowing things to happen to me; I take charge and begin to organise my own future. I am concerned about my mother's health so soon decide that my dream must wait a while because I want to be free to look after her back home in Victoria if and when it becomes necessary. This doesn't deter me because I know that a lot of planning will be needed before I can leave Australia for France.

I buy a big red book with pages in alphabetical order and in this I write and paste anything that might be of use to me when I am ready to begin – lists of books and publishers, articles about books, art, music and small business, in both French and English – all kinds of things relating to the promotion of Australian books in France. In the 'A' section I have information about such diverse subjects as the Australia Council, the Australian Society of Authors, the Australian Booksellers' Association, the Alliance Française, Aboriginal culture (subdivided into art, music and books), audio books, Australian art in general, Asia, American connections, animals . . .

I already own and have read a good collection of books by Australian authors and now I set out to expand my knowledge of Australian literature by reading all the reviews I can find and by searching for books in second-hand book-shops. Browsing gives me great pleasure but it's even more rewarding if one has a purpose.

Some years after I was divorced I moved, with a friend, from Melbourne to Sydney. This was a major upheaval and at that stage of my life I could not have done it alone. My close friend, Pauline Ferguson, managed to get me leave without pay for a year so that I had the option of returning to work in Melbourne if things didn't work out well in Sydney. As always, the most difficult objects to move were my greatly-treasured old Lipp piano, which is an upright grand and therefore very tall and very heavy, and the dozens of boxes of books. My books are an eclectic mix of novels, biographies and autobiographies, poetry, art books, travel books (especially about France) and many books about music and musicians.

When my children were young we lived in Hamilton, in the western district of Victoria, and eagerly devoured the Mary Martin and Academic Remainders book lists. The highlights of each month were the parcels of books sent by post from these two great mail-order bookshops. During the twelve years we lived in Hamilton I taught Music, French and English at Maryknoll College, so was always looking for books to keep up to date with these subjects. During the sixties my students and I had a wonderful time experimenting with R. Murray Schafer's *Ear Cleaning* (1967) ideas, such as creating and notating soundscapes using all kinds of 'instruments' found in our everyday environment. I gleaned these ideas from books, as they certainly weren't part of the music course at Melbourne University in the fifties. I still own most of the books from that period because I'm not very good at discarding them; those books I love become old friends and I want to have them around me.

During my first year of living in Sydney I continued teaching and spent every weekend looking at books just because I loved them but now that I have my own bookshop plan, I am also interested in how bookshops operate – the layout, window displays, lighting, attitudes of staff, book readings, advertising, promotional ideas: anything and everything which might help me in Paris.

I become interested in translation and wonder how many Australian books have been translated into French. It would be good to be able to sell Australian books in both English and French but discovering how many Australian books have been translated into French proves difficult so I decide this will have to wait until I can go to Paris, where they are published, to undertake some market research. Nevertheless, I now search through French magazines at the State Library of New South Wales and keep a lookout for mentions of translations in the local press. My interest in French translation triggers an interest in translation in general and it seems that here in Australia not many books are published in languages other than English despite the fact that our population is composed of many people whose mother tongue is not English.

The bookshop is a long-term plan and I know that it might be ten years before I am ready to do even the market research. To keep myself busy I spend six months working on a book about Australian history through music. The educational publisher at Cambridge University Press expresses a strong interest and sends me copies of four very good reviews he has received from people who have read my proposal. When this falls in a heap I contact Lyn Spender of the Australian Society of Authors. She is wonderfully supportive and helpful so I join the ASA and, to my surprise, am admitted as a full member because of the educational writing I have done, both in Victoria and New South Wales and because of the two Australian song books a friend and I have had published.

As part of my Paris bookshop preparation I try to keep up to date with contemporary Australian writing by reading *Australian Book Review* and *Australian Bookseller and Publisher* as well as any music and art magazines I can find at my local library. There's a lot to learn and I am becoming more and more engrossed in the task I have undertaken.

But although the dream bookshop is always on my mind, it still seems a long way off because I know that I can't make any major decisions and must go ahead with my life in Sydney until such time as my mother needs me. Apart from my teaching colleagues, some of whom have become friends, I don't know many people in Sydney and feel the need to expand my circle and, at the same time, bring myself up to date with current academic thinking. So I enrol for a Master's degree at the University of New South Wales, choosing to study Ethnomusicology because it is a relatively new discipline and was not available when I studied music at Melbourne University in the 1950s.

It is nearly thirty years since I was a university student and I'm now in my fifties so at first I'm very nervous about my ability to cope. So much has changed – libraries have become computerised, information technology seems over-whelming at first and the students all look so much younger. The course I have chosen combines the preparation of a thesis with several lectures a week.

At our first Ethnomusicology lecture we listen to music from a number of different Australian Aboriginal communities and I am ashamed at my lack of knowledge concerning the culture of Indigenous Australians. When I was six years old I had an Aboriginal playmate, but never enquired about her background; we just enjoyed playing together without thinking about anything else. In the 1960s I taught secondary school students the poetry of Kath Walker, now known as Oodgeroo Noonucal, and I also taught a few Aboriginal songs arranged by white Australians, but that was all. My lecturer, who has been closely associated with the people of Arnhem Land, now attempts to remedy this lack of background knowledge as well as teach me how to recognise the characteristics of the music of many different Indigenous communities and to transcribe their music directly from original recordings. All the time I am studying, I think how the things I'm learning might help with the bookshop: my increased understanding of Indigenous culture should certainly be an asset in promoting Australian arts in France.

After a year of teaching all day and studying at night I decide to give up full-time teaching and look for some free-lance work. Some of my friends and family are horrified but I feel that it's time for a change and, eventually, when it's time to follow my bookshop dream, I'll have to resign anyway. I have taught in secondary schools for twenty-three years and loved it. If I could begin again I would do the same thing because, for me, nothing is more rewarding than engaging with young people and encouraging them to expand their horizons.

Amazingly, within a week I have enough work to get by – to my delight and astonishment I am offered five hours of teaching in the Music Department at the University of New South Wales (where I am studying) and the principal of Kincoppal Rose Bay School offers me a contract to produce a musical for the school, starting almost immediately. Within a few months I receive other employment offers, teaching singing, piano and harmony, and soon find myself just as busy as when I worked full-time. I have to cut back the work in order to complete my thesis and continue with my bookshop preparations.

During the final year of my Master's degree I am offered a job at Da Capo music bookshop in Glebe and discover just how much I love the whole bookshop experience – because of my background, selling books about music to other aficionados is a special delight and, as well as the sales experience, I learn about cataloguing, buying and pricing. It's a wonderful shop and my time there reinforces my Paris dream.

The next year I work for a Sydney advertising agency, but when the owner asks me to come back the following year as office manager I politely decline. The experience gained there in sales and marketing will also be useful in Paris.

In the early 1990s I almost give up my bookshop idea because I fall in love with a man called William. He is a great reader and once owned a small, independent bookshop in Sydney. We have a lot in common and life is never dull because we both like talking and debating. The idea of having a life companion is tempting and it is wonderful to feel admired and nurtured so I invite William to come down to Melbourne with me to meet my children and my parents. This is not a huge success; he feels that I love my children more than I love him. I try to explain that maternal love is very different from mutual adult love but he has no children so cannot really understand. He becomes possessive and jealous of my relationships with other people. This kind of love feels claustrophobic so I finally decide that I am not prepared to again place my whole happiness in someone else's hands. Strangely, I have not told him about my bookshop dream because I doubt that he would leave Sydney, where he has a permanent job and, importantly for him, daily help from an old and trusted friend. Because of a childhood injury he is unable to drive a car so needs help with shopping and travelling to work. I would have to give up my Paris dreaming to be with William and in the end I cannot do so.

After about twelve months of being very angry with me, William forgives me and we remain friends. I now tell him of my bookshop dream and he understands perfectly because of his own bookshop experience. He understands my longing and helps me with ideas and suggestions for the opening stock. He is not a wealthy man so I am moved when he tells me that if I should ever need money urgently he will send it.

William and I spend a lot of time discussing what kinds of books might appeal to the French; I decide it would be a good idea to sell Australian books in both French and English as I have been told that no other Parisian bookshop is doing this; the elegant and legendary Galignani's in rue de Rivoli sells books in both English and French but they don't seem to stock any Australian authors.

One day William tells me he has met a charming Frenchwoman called Josie and has suggested to her that she teach me French in exchange for piano lessons. This arrangement works well and Josie and I become close friends. She is a strong, intelligent woman who has worked very hard to build a successful life in Australia. I admire her attitude to life and she becomes an inspiration to me. We always speak in French when we are together and she gives me insights into the French way of thinking as well as telling me about some of the difficulties of living and working in another country.

⁖⊙ ⊙⁖

For almost ten years I work and plan and when time seems to be passing too slowly, I am supported by those closest to me. There is, as well, my dream travelling-trunk that stands beside the piano. Now, more than thirty-five years after I bought it, I know I won't be travelling by ship, but it's still a powerful symbol.

One day I receive the phone call from my father that I have long been expecting. He asks me to come home to Victoria to help nurse my mother. I wanted to go earlier but he is an independent man and proud of being able to manage on his own. She is refusing to eat, so I forget about everything else and spend the next six months on the family farm. It is a time I will remember with both sadness and joy, because I become closer to my mother as both she and I grow older, so it is good to be with her at the end of her life.

When it is all over I tell my father about my plan. He is

at first shocked but then says he understands, because he too chose a new lifestyle at sixty years of age. I am aware that he would like me to stay on the farm to look after him and I struggle with my conscience before realising that I can't do it. I will always have some regrets about this but I have put so much time and energy into the bookshop plan that I cannot turn back now and I can't return to the submissive role he would expect of me.

After so many years, what was at first a whimsical idea has become much, much more. Through my research, I am now aware of how little is being done to promote Australian arts, both nationally and internationally. Australia is part of the international community but, with a few exceptions, we rarely make headlines overseas and if we do the image conveyed is often clichéd – stories of sea, sun, sand and sport and a few strange animals thrown in. If you mention snow on mountains and the variety of the Australian landscape, the French will look at you with disbelief and question your integrity – '*Ce n'est pas vrai!*' (That can't be true!) French people are more aware of the Australian cinema than they are of art, literature or music, but the idea that we might have thinkers and writers with something worthwhile to say doesn't seem to be considered compatible with the easy-going, 'good sports' image the French have of the average Australian.

I am now convinced that an Australian bookshop in Paris

is a necessity rather than simply a change of lifestyle for me. I have chosen Paris because I know the language and, as a result of several visits to my son David, who has studied and worked in Paris for a long time, I already have friends and contacts there. Because David has successfully become part of the Parisian artistic community, I feel more at home in Paris than in any other European city. Some kind of shopfront in other major cities of the world would be a great way of promoting a more accurate image of Australia to other countries but, as I don't have the financial means to establish worldwide cultural centres, a small bookshop in Paris seems a good way to begin.

I decide that before making the final decision to go ahead with the bookshop plan, I must live in Paris for at least six months to do some market research and, just as importantly, to gauge whether I can live there alone. Although David is based in Paris, he is a musician and often travelling so I need to be as self-reliant as possible.

My head's in a whirl. My Sydney terrace house is rented for a year and David finds me an apartment in Avenue Parmentier, Paris, which I can lease for seven months. Somehow everything is ready. I say my goodbyes to family and friends and then I am on the plane, full of anticipation and excitement, feeling somewhat surreal, as we fly for five hours over miles and miles of red, cracked earth until at last we reach the sea and Australia is left behind.

Chapter 4

FORGING LINKS

'He who draws noble delights from sentiments of poetry is a true poet, though he has never written a line in all his life.'

George Sand

PARIS, 1994

Twenty-four hours after leaving Australia, I am in Paris, being welcomed in French by the owner of David's local Vietnamese restaurant. When David made the booking he told him I was coming and he seems impressed that my son has met me at the airport and brought me here to eat. He makes a long speech to that effect, in which he asks quite vehemently whether I realise how fortunate I am to have an adult son who will give up some time for me. Feeling jet-lagged and not quite sure what to say, I reply, slowly and in my very best French, that I am indeed blessed in having such a caring son. I use the word *gentille* (nice) because I don't know how to say 'caring', but as a first conversation with a native this trip, I think I manage well.

I'm curious about why the restaurateur feels so strongly about this – perhaps he has had problems with his own children – I would like to ask him about his family but my French is not up to it and, besides, it is probably not done. I have been warned about the importance of *la politesse* and I am not yet sure of the nuances of polite conversation, which seem to vary greatly depending upon circumstances and how well you know the company you keep. It is clear that David eats here regularly and that the owner is sufficiently fond of him to make sure I understand and appreciate my good luck in being his mother.

With a polite '*au revoir*' and '*merci, monsieur*', after we finish our meal we go to the apartment David has found for me in Avenue Parmentier, close to Métro Saint-Ambroise in the 11th arrondissement. I am pleased to find that this is not a tourist area because I want to experience, as much as possible, the French way of living. This part of Avenue Parmentier is within walking distance of the hustle and bustle of Bastille and République, the leafy charm of the much-visited Père Lachaise cemetery and the busy restaurants and bars of rue Oberkampf and rue Ménilmontant, but it is itself a quiet street with rather ordinary shops and offices interspersed with Haussmann-style apartments.

My temporary home is in one of these apartments, which were built by Baron Haussmann in the second half of the nineteenth century in order to 'tidy up' Paris. He got rid of most of the twisting old laneways and replaced them with tree-lined boulevards and elegant houses. The houses are nearly all six storeys high with attics under the roof featuring dormer windows – these attics were originally built for the servants but most of them are now rented out to students or struggling artists who still refer to them as *chambres de bonne* (maids' rooms). The front rooms are usually decorated with small, wrought-iron balconies in front of French windows but in my apartment the balcony is really only a flower-box. Happily, it contains some red geraniums and these, together with the owner's indoor plants, create a warm, welcoming atmosphere. The apartment is built around what looks like an interior courtyard so there are plenty of windows, all with their little planters.

There is no lift in this building so, as we climb the worn wooden stairs, I tell myself that it is fortunate that my apartment is on the second floor and not the sixth. It is winter but the whole building is warmed by some kind of central heating, which I suppose must be controlled from the basement. Despite the rather stark appearance of the stairwell we feel cosy as soon as we enter the building. By Paris standards this apartment is quite large – there is even room for a table in the kitchen, an unusual feature in most small Parisian apartments. The lounge–dining area and the bedroom are comfortably furnished with CD player, television and books. The atmosphere is not so very different from that of my Sydney terrace house so almost immediately I begin to feel *chez-moi* in these rooms.

The young woman who owns the apartment has gone to South America for seven months, so the length of my stay is decided for me. She has written a meticulous inventory of every single item in the apartment, right down to the last battered saucepan, and has left the name, address and phone number of a friend I can contact if I have any problems. But before I have a chance to have any problems the friend contacts me. He turns out to be a charming young man called Sebastien who lives close by and loves choral music. He invites me to come along to some of the concerts in which he is performing and there I meet a mixture of people of all ages – artists, musicians, business people and students. I'm forced to speak French because Sebastien and his friends don't speak English. I feel like an outsider because my French is not as fluent as I would like but, nevertheless, learn a lot about how the French behave by quietly observing how these people interact. At the same time I realise how inadequate some migrants must feel when they arrive in Australia with little or no English. Having worked as a voluntary teacher of English to migrants in Melbourne during the seventies I already have some sensitivity towards their situation and still remember some horrific stories of the displacement felt by some of my students. I will never forget the lonely wife of a wealthy Japanese businessman who jumped to her death from the balcony of her luxurious Toorak home. I repeatedly tell myself how fortunate I am in already having some links with Parisians because, despite its beauty, I am sure Paris could be a very lonely place without friends or family.

During my first few days in Paris, everything seems stark to me and I notice things with unusual clarity, especially the differences between my life here and in Sydney. The everyday details of life seem more formal here, right down to the polite *bonjour* or *bonsoir* to fellow tenants as we pass on the stairway. Simple things like going to the *supermarché* are big experiences and the fantastic food displays seem to emphasise the differences. Eating and drinking are almost art forms here and I love being surprised by quaint little cafés and bistros. The whole atmosphere seems more gentle and considered, especially in this quiet part of Paris. The busy city of Sydney and its beautiful harbour seem a long way away.

I feel distanced from Australia but at the same time I don't yet feel a part of my new home, especially as I'm not confident about speaking French fluently. But within a few weeks life becomes 'normal' and I begin to feel that I am part of the community centred around Métro Saint-Ambroise. The local butcher earnestly tells me which cuts of meat I should buy to make a genuine *boeuf bourguignon* and the small *supermarché* next door, with its cheap but good wines, cheeses and *pâtés*, becomes familiar. There is a *tabac* just over the road and several little bars, cafés and restaurants which I can visit if I don't feel like cooking or am in need of company.

It's not long before I have a favourite neighbourhood restaurant – En Faim, in rue Saint-Ambroise. It's the kind of genuine local restaurant that tourists hope they will discover, off the beaten track and not expensive, especially if you like *raclette*, *fondue* and other hearty dishes like *blanquette de veau.* The restaurant's tiny façade is decorated with lace curtains, giving it a provincial, postcard look. There are only eight tables, covered with printed tablecloths and the young couple who run the restaurant are relaxed and friendly; their easy charm has attracted a number of 'regulars'. People from all walks of life eat at En Faim so I often go there alone to people-watch or read the newspapers in true French tradition. I admit to a little eavesdropping as well, mainly to improve my French but also to get the feel of things.

The French owners of En Faim tell me that a parliamentarian, M. Toubon, is trying to forbid the use of English words, especially in government departments and public places, so they have crossed out the word 'brownie' from the menu and substituted '*toubon*'. They are pleased with their little joke and I am very happy to understand it, because it's often difficult to understand jokes in a foreign language and I have already attended a few gatherings where I simply couldn't follow the jokes or the current slang. I feel very inadequate on such occasions, but am slowly broadening my vocabulary.

One evening at En Faim I meet Sandra, a tall, elegant, beautifully dressed American woman who has written a series of books called *Cheap Eats in Paris* and *Cheap Sleeps in Paris*. She has written the same for Italy, London and Hawaii and now has what seems to me an enviable life-style which consists of doing the rounds of those cities to check the places already mentioned and to delete them or add new ones, depending on how she finds them.

Sandra and I become friends and I am delighted to have met her because it will be good to have a network of friends waiting for me if and when I return to establish the bookshop. Sometimes I accompany her on visits to 'old' and 'new' restaurants, which I find fascinating because restaurants are marvellous places for people-watching and I become familiar with her favourite eating-places. Sandra has travelled widely throughout Europe, Asia and the Middle East and has lived in Paris, Prague and Singapore, so for me, a newcomer to living and eating in France, she is a mine of useful information.

The days are mainly spent walking the streets of Paris, absorbing the atmosphere and visiting the bookshops, art galleries and museums of each quartier, but despite my friendship with Sandra I am sometimes lonely because David is very busy and works long hours. This means that if I want to see him it is usually for a late dinner appointment at one of the many restaurants popular with musicians and theatre people. On these occasions I meet his friends and am able to observe and experience another section of the Paris community.

David is currrently the musical director of a *spectacle* (show) called *Cabaret Sauvage*, to be presented next year in a famous old *chapiteau* (tent) at Le Parc de la Villette. He explains to me that the park is a huge area on the north-eastern side of Paris constructed to replace the former central slaughterhouse and livestock market. It is surrounded by canals and consists of hectares of gardens as well as the Géode (a huge hemispheric movie theatre), the Cité des Sciences (the French national technology museum), Zénith (a famous rock hall), a huge building used for *salons* (trade fairs), the Cité de la Musique and the new Paris national music school. And, of course, there is the large space where the *chapiteau* will be erected next year for the *Cabaret Sauvage* show. The management of La Villette is open to all new forms of creation including street arts and the 'new circus' – it sounds very enticing to me and I look forward to going there one day.

David tells me that *Cabaret Sauvage* could be described as a kind of 'cabaret circus' with clowns and acrobats as well as music and dance – a recreation of the travelling cabarets of the 1920s and '30s. He shows me photos of the *chapiteau*, which is the most amazing tent I have ever seen. It has an Art Nouveau look and is made up of varnished wood panels, lots of mirrors and red fabric and a bar. The only thing that's canvas is the roof. It's really a portable dance-hall and immediately evokes a cabaret atmosphere. I think it's wonderful and feel very sad that I won't be in Paris in 1995 when the show starts. When David throws a party I meet some of the *Cabaret Sauvage* performers, including a young singer called Belle du Berry who seems to hold a special place in his affection.

Through David I meet some of Paris' favourite musicians, such as legendary African musician Manu Dibango and the French singer Arthur H, who is popular with both Parisians and French expats in Australia. I learn that he is the son of the much-admired singer Jacques Higelin, who is currently performing at the Cirque d'Hiver. When David takes me to see live music, we go backstage and meet some of the artists and their families and I gradually develop an affinity with them and their admirers. It helps in conversations at dinner-tables if you know something of popular Parisian musicians, actors, cinema directors and film stars and I am sure this background knowledge will be useful if and when my dream bookshop becomes a reality. I hope that an understanding of contemporary French culture will help me to create a meeting-place and a springboard from which I can introduce some Australian equivalents.

၏ ၆

At a party one evening David introduces me to a young Frenchwoman who is the life of the party – vivacious and radiating energy, she seems to know everyone and is interested in everything. She takes me under her wing, introduces me to her friends, adds some colourful words to my French vocabulary and takes me to places I could never have discovered on my own. Her name is Nicole, and she is *une vraie parisienne* (a true Parisienne). She was born in Paris, whereas many people who work in Paris come from the provinces and often have an apartment in Paris and their family home in the country which they return to most weekends.

Nicole lives in Montmartre, not far from Métro Les Abbesses. The entrance to this métro is a lovely example of architect Hector Guimaud's Art Nouveau style and is a Parisian landmark. Nicole and I wander the back streets behind Sacré Cœur and she teaches me so much about Montmartre and its history that I begin to experience it as a village. Our favourite walk begins at the foot of rue Lepic, a narrow street that climbs up to rue des Abbesses from Métro Blanche. There are all kinds of foods for sale and there is even a butcher's shop with a gilded horse's head above the doorway, indicating a *boucherie chevaline* (some people still eat the sweet-tasting horsemeat, so I'm told, but the same people are horrified at the thought of eating kangaroo meat). Already my head is back in old Paris when Montmartre was a country village on the outskirts of the city, with vineyards and windmills. We cross rue des Abbesses and rue Lepic curves on and upwards, around the side of the hill, in the shape of a large horseshoe. This part of the street is usually deserted, perhaps because it is rather steep; I think most people must climb the steps up to the front of Sacré Cœur with its crowds of tourists and vendors selling all kinds of kitschy souvenirs. These steps are, in fact, much steeper than the quiet back streets of Montmartre.

We pass the Moulin de la Galette, the last of more than thirty Montmartre windmills, much painted by such artists as Renoir, Van Gogh and Toulouse-Lautrec, and then walk through a very small park where we see Saint Denis holding his head in his hands – Montmartre (the martyr's mountain) is named after him and, according to Nicole, legend says that after he was beheaded he walked on to the north of Paris with his mitred head in his hands until he reached the spot where the basilica Saint Denis now stands. We leave him in his serene little garden next to the children's sandpits and go up some steep steps and then down to a raised terrace that leads to a little square with a bust of Dalida, the famous Egyptian singer. It's a beautiful work and I have the feeling she is at peace here in this quiet little corner of Montmartre.

We continue climbing until finally we reach the last of the old vineyards. Now we really are in old Montmartre, where the streets have not much changed since they were painted in the nineteenth century. Nicole shows me La Maison Rose (the pink house), which I have seen in postcards of Utrillo's paintings. The postcards seem to spring to life, especially when we reach the last of the old vineyards and, over on the corner of rue des Saules and rue Saint-Vincent, find Le Lapin Agile, a cabaret once owned by the entertainer Aristide Bruant. Nicole tells me that it was once known as the 'Café des Assassins' (for obvious reasons) and it's only tourists who come here now, in the evenings. On the days we pass by, it too seems peaceful and calm.

Nicole says that I should come back in October when they celebrate the annual harvest of the grapes with a big festival – there's a procession with bands and marching girls and people dressed in revolutionary costumes, and lots of wine. She loves these celebrations and we join in whenever there's the chance to do so. Nicole also teaches me some of Serge Gainsbourg's songs – I think she relates to his wicked sense of humour even though some might see him as a misogynist, with such lines as *'sois belle et tais-toi'* (politely translated: 'be beautiful and keep quiet'). We investigate lots of little bars and bistros in the area, many of which are well known to Nicole. It's wonderful exploring Montmartre with her and I am delighted to include her in my network of friends who, I hope, will be waiting in Paris when I return.

Living in the same district are Alan and Gordon, who are friends of both Nicole and David. They love throwing parties and, on one occasion, when they have obtained some special sausages from Munich, they invite a group of friends to share them. I phone to offer help with the cooking and am asked to prepare *chou rouge* (red cabbage) for twelve people. I have absolutely no idea how to do this so I look up a recipe in the little cookery book I have bought to familiarise myself with basic French cuisine. The recipe is called *Chou rouge aux pommes* (red cabbage with apples) and as I've never made it before I allow the whole day for the experiment. I slice four onions and wash four red cabbages under running water. Next I rinse the cabbages in vinegar and allow them to drain. So far, so good. When I think they are dry I cut each cabbage into four pieces and remove the hard centres. I cut them into thin strips, carefully removing any hard pieces of the leaves.

I sauté the sliced onions, then mix in the cabbage leaves, add twelve tablespoons of wine vinegar and stir. 'Bubble, bubble, toil and trouble,' I think. If the mixture becomes too thick (and it does) I am permitted to thin it with water or *bouillon*. As I don't have *bouillon* in my larder, I thin it a little with some water. Then I add the ubiquitous *bouquet garni* (a little bundle of parsley, thyme and crushed bay leaves) and cook the mixture for about an hour, until the cabbage is soft.

Removing the saucepan from the heat, I peel, core and dice sixteen apples and mix them with 120 grams of red currant jelly (bought from the *supermarché*), salt and pepper. I add this mixture to the cabbage, cover it with a lid and must cook it very gently until the apples are soft. The recipe says 'about thirty minutes' but I've multiplied the recipe by four so the cooking time takes much longer than indicated. I feel as though I've done a day's work.

At the end I have an enormous potful of a rich, fragrant, jammy substance so, armed with a large, heavy saucepan full of red cabbage, I set out to travel by métro from Saint-Ambroise to Les Abbesses. This is the first time I've actually taken the métro to Les Abbesses (I have only admired the entrance from the street before). I notice the lifts but decide to use the stairs. This is a bad decision. I didn't realise how deeply this railway line is buried in the base of the mountain which is Montmartre. Later I learn that Les Abbesses is the deepest metro in Paris; the metro exit is about halfway up the mountain. Sacré Cœur, with its gleaming white domes, stands on its peak and is a familiar part of the Paris skyline.

Clutching my heavy load I climb an interminable number of steps and, to make matters worse, I am early. Parisians never arrive early. I have been invited for eight o'clock and it's only 7.30 now, but my red cabbage is too heavy for me to hang around for the sake of politeness.

When I arrive at the building where Alan and Gordon live, I find a code is required before I can enter the building. I am exhausted and can walk no further in search of the nearest phone-box, so, in desperation, I throw pebbles at what I hope is my hosts' window until eventually they hear me and press the buzzer to let me in. Finding people in

Paris is sometimes a kind of treasure hunt because you might have a code to enter the main door but then there can be two or three staircases to choose from and sometimes a second code. It can be nerve-racking. What to do if you don't have the code?

When I finally arrive at the party, Alan and Gordon and their French friends are so impressed at my knowing how to cook *chou rouge* successfully that I can't bring myself to admit it's my first effort.

It's a very merry evening with hearty food, good conversation and lots of music. We begin the meal with an array of *pâtés, terrines, saucisson sec* and *cornichons*. The chutney-like *chou rouge* goes well with the main course, sausages from Munich, which are followed by salads, cheeses and fruit. Various musicians take turns in playing and at one stage, suitably primed by wine, we gather around the piano for a good old-fashioned sing-a-long. Food, wine and a love of talking – especially about cinema, books and music – are essential components of most Parisian dinner parties, and these are some of the reasons why I love Paris and its people and already feel thrilled at the idea of living here. Parisians can argue quite vehemently and interrupt each other when they become excited, but it is rarely personal and after the debates conclude everyone seems to be relaxed and smiling.

On an earlier trip to France, I met a Parisian couple, Jacques and Vivienne, with whom I have been corresponding. Now they invite me to dinner and make me feel very welcome. They live in the north-eastern part of Paris, near the Parc de la Villette, and on walks around the area they show me the Canal Saint-Martin and its environs. Jacques is an American who came to Paris in 1968 to work for UNESCO and Vivienne is French. Both are outgoing, ebullient people and are determined that I will enjoy Paris. They introduce me to their favourite places and with them I discover *les huitres à volonté* (all the oysters you can eat) at the Brasserie de Clichy as well as traditional foods at other ancient bistros, with their original zinc counters. On our frequent strolls they introduce me to numerous out-of-the-way village-like quartiers such as la Butte-aux-Cailles, with its little workers' houses, cobbled streets and gardens. I begin to know more of the villages of Paris.

Vivienne tells me how to obtain free concert and theatre tickets given by the magazine *Télérama* to readers who have time to wait in line, and I quickly learn how to hold my own in a Paris queue. This is not easy: the queues are very disorderly and everyone seems to think they have a reason to jump ahead. If you aren't careful they push in or stand beside someone near the front and gradually edge in. If this happens the others shout angrily, '*La queue! La queue!*' It can be entertaining but you mustn't show your amusement, as people are very serious about what they regard as their individual rights. If it's not a long line it is quite acceptable to run to the back and queue again for more tickets until they run out.

Another old friend, Valerie, is the American/Australian agent for a well-known violinist, Ivry Gitlis, and she too is living here. Now she shows me her Paris: it is Valerie who first introduces me to the pleasure of watching the sun go down over drinks at Café Marly, opposite the Pyramide du Louvre. We celebrate her birthday there, watching the colours of the setting sun reflected from the walls of the glass pyramid. This gradually becomes one of my special places in Paris.

When I'm not with David and my friends, I have long hours alone which I fill by reading and by exploring Paris – seeking out anything and everything relevant to the opening of an Australian bookshop here and to feeling at home in this city. By now, with a widening circle of people with whom I am comfortable and happy, I decide to begin the serious part of my market research. I need to discover whether there really is a market for Australian books in Paris, and whether there is likely to be any support from either French or Australian bureaucrats.

Chapter 5

MARKET RESEARCH

'Of all the inanimate objects, of all men's creations, books are the nearest to us, for they contain our very thoughts, our ambitions, our indignations, our illusions, our fidelity to the truth, and our persistent leaning towards error. But most of all they resemble us in their precarious hold on life.'

Joseph Conrad

PARIS, 1994

In the course of my research I visit specialist bookshops and cultural centres and contact anyone who seems to display an interest in Australian books. I comb the newspapers and *les annonces* in expat magazines such as *Paris Free Voice, Boulevarde* and *FUSAC*, and gradually discover that it is still very difficult to find Australian books in either the Anglo or French bookshops.

French people tell me they would be interested in reading Australian authors in translation but they have difficulty knowing which books *are* Australian because, in bookshop displays, Australian authors are usually shelved with American and English writers and on the cover or title page it usually just says *'traduit de l'anglais'*. More recent publications have *'traduit de l'anglais (Australie)'* and this is helpful, but the would-be reader still has to search for the Australian books. There is a real need for a space which could display the latest Australian books for people to touch, look at, discuss and then, hopefully, buy.

In my bookshop, I decide, I will place English and French editions of the same book side by side on the bookshelves so that the customers can then choose immediately whether they want to read the book in French, in English or in both languages.

I find so few Australian books available in either the Anglo or French-speaking general bookshops that I begin to look at second-hand books and find translations of books by Patrick White, Colleen McCullough, Morris West, Arthur Upfield, Nevil Shute and Nancy Cato. White won the Nobel prize so that explains his popularity but I'm not sure why these particular authors are comparatively well known in France when there are so many other good writers. Occasionally I come across a copy of one of these books in English but mostly they are translations. I ask myself how these books arrived in France and note their names in my Big Red Book for further investigation.

I visit the Australian Embassy in Paris because I have read about the Australia France Foundation (AFF), which was established, and I quote from the 1993–94 Report, 'as the major element of Australia's official contribution to the celebration of the bicentenary of the French Revolution and of the Declaration of the Rights of Man and of the Citizen'. It is a public trust fund with an initial contribution of AU$1.1 million by the Australian Government 'to promote knowledge of Australia in France across the broadest possible range of activities, including the arts, science and technology, Australian studies and sport'.

I think an Australian bookshop in Paris would fit very well into these categories because all of those activities mentioned above could be promoted through books. My research reveals that the responsibility for administering the Australia France Foundation's programme has recently been transferred to the Australian Embassy in Paris so I phone to make an appointment with the person presently in charge.

This is the first time in my life that I have visited an embassy so I arrive a little ahead of time, not quite knowing what to expect. The Embassy is imposing and passing through the inspection facilities at the entrance door is a new experience for me. I am a little nervous but the guard is very friendly and asks me to wait while he lets the Cultural Officer know I'm here.

This building, designed by Australian architect Harry Seidler, has an enormous entry hall which feels quite daunting when it's empty. (There is a joke among expats here: 'Why is the Australian Embassy in Paris similar to Australia? Because it's large on the outside and empty in the inside.') I sit and wait. Eventually the Cultural Officer appears and ushers me through a second hall and then into the library. It is a very brief meeting and she doesn't offer me a seat. After I have explained my project she dismisses me, saying that the Australia France Foundation only helps people who are 'important or well-known'.

Deflated, I quickly make my departure. This woman leaves the job a few weeks later, which could partly explain her lack of interest in my plans. Or perhaps she is just tired of people coming along with bright ideas and asking for help. I don't really have the chance to explain in detail how I would go about transforming my ideas into reality and I don't have enough experience with embassies to know that I should ask to see the Cultural Attaché, as opposed to the Cultural Officer. I know from my research in Australia that my plans are not sufficiently advanced to ask for help from Austrade (the Australian Trade Delegation), and, in any case, I know my proposed business-plan does not meet their criteria, specifically the condition that AU$30,000 be spent on publicity. It seems that I have come to a dead end, at least as far as help from the Australia France Foundation is concerned.

ᴄᴏ☙ ❧ᴏᴏ

I am disappointed, but not defeated. Next I contact the office-bearers of the various French 'Australophile satellites' which revolve around the Embassy and whose members, I am told, go to all Australian functions. As I get to know them, each of these groups seems to me to be proprietorial and competitive about their relationships with Australia, some more so than others. It intrigues me and I wonder whether the same thing happens in other countries.

In my Big Red Book, among the newspaper clippings, there is an article from an Australian newspaper about a French couple who are interested in Australian literature so I phone them and am invited to afternoon tea. I haven't visited this part of Paris before and am amazed to see that they seem to occupy a whole house with a beautiful garden, almost a *maison de campagne* (country house). Most of the people I have visited so far live in apartments and the wealthier ones own two or even three floors of an apartment building. This is the first self-contained house I have visited and it is a peaceful oasis on the outskirts of a crowded city.

As yet I have never been received by royalty or by an ambassador, but the afternoon is just as I have imagined such an occasion. Madame is an attentive hostess and they are politely interested in my plans, but not as excited as I had hoped they might be. This is my first visit to a more traditional French household and I tell myself not to expect too much from a first meeting. I have mainly been mixing with either French artists of one kind or another, who seem to have broken away from traditional social structures, or with a few American or British expats who are quick to make friends with like-minded people, and I have forgotten the clear distinction made between friends and acquaintances by those French families who still observe the ancient rituals.

My host and hostess are perfectly charming and present me with a cup of tea but they don't have one themselves. I find this unusual because, in my experience, if someone has an appointment and tea is offered, everyone partakes. *Eh bien*, I think, I am in Paris. Perhaps things are done differently here. They are very formal and I realise that I should have come with a letter of introduction from someone 'well known'.

Monsieur and Madame tell me they have worked for years to promote Australian books in France but they really can't help me, except by providing a list of some of the books already translated into French, with the names of their translators. I am very pleased to have this list because up until now my Big Red Book has contained only a very short list of translations. Theirs is not extensive but it is much more detailed than mine. I admire their wonderful collection of Australian books, thank them for their hospitality and depart.

They seemed pessimistic about my idea but I'm still undaunted. At least the fact that they have already worked at promoting Australian books in France gives me something to build on.

The representatives of some other groups I meet enthusiastically offer to help in any way possible once the bookshop is established. Others adopt a 'wait and see' attitude, which is very sensible of them, I suppose. The Australian owner of a British bookshop in Bordeaux replies to my letter, telling me that if I try to sell Australian books in France I will break my heart and lose my money. When I visit him he doesn't say much but clearly believes there is no demand for Australian books.

Some time later I discover a little café called the Sydney Coffee Shop and the owner and I become friends. Barbara is an Australian who came to Paris specifically to open this café so she has already been through the daunting experience of dealing with foreign bureaucracy. I hope I can learn from her experiences so visit her often. I love the walk home in the evening or early morning from the Coffee Shop in rue Lacépède to my home in the 11th, which takes me along rue des Fosses-Saint-Bernard, across the very tip of Île Saint-Louis via the Pont Sully and straight up Boulevard Henri IV to Bastille. Then it is a brisk trot up rue de la Roquette and I am in Avenue Parmentier. All the important monuments are beautifully lit and it's like strolling through a gigantic theatre set. I never tire of Paris by night and become accustomed to walking around at all hours. I walk quickly and purposefully because I have discovered that if I linger it is regarded as a sign that I want company.

Barbara tells me a lot about setting up a business in France as a foreigner and I often accompany her when she goes on 'official' errands, thus gaining some idea of what may lie ahead for me. She introduces me to her contact at the French Chamber of Commerce, who is very charming and expresses interest in my project.

The Sydney Coffee Shop is a welcoming little café, with its smell of hot pastry and coffee, its curved counter in polished wood, a few enticing tables and chairs and a

Foster's sign hanging outside. It seems to attract homesick Australians as well as the curious French. One of Barbara's regular customers is a young lawyer from Sydney who comes every morning for a cooked breakfast of bacon and eggs with toast. He doesn't like French food. The Sydney Coffee Shop also offers hot meat pies and, of course, Foster's beer, both of which are a novelty for the French.

Despite these attractions, Barbara tells me that she is having difficulty in making a go of it and I decide that one of the reasons may be that although many people visit the Mouffetard, the interesting and colourful mediaeval street at the top of the hill, they don't pass by the Sydney Coffee Shop because they usually walk up rue Cardinal Lemoine or approach *La Mouffe* from Mont Saint-Geneviève. A central position is, obviously, very important, so my vision of a quiet little bookshop in an out-of-the way corner of Paris is rapidly disappearing. I will have to search for a very central position in order to attract both busy Parisians and tourists.

Through Barbara and the Sydney Coffee Shop I meet two Frenchwomen who tell me they love Australia and would like to create a cultural centre with its own magazine. Barbara will be the editor of the magazine and the librarian from the Embassy will help. We have several meetings and I tell them my plans but despite their enthusiasm, neither of them has any financial backing. I decide to keep in touch with them but to work alone.

In my Big Red Book I have pasted an article about Australian studies in France so I contact some of the universities who offer courses with Australian content. They all say they are desperate for books and textbooks and are excited at the idea of being able to see the books before buying them. I suggest reading the *Australian Book Review* as an introduction to Australian writing but many of them say that their budgets are small and they cannot afford the subscription. I will investigate the feasibility of selling journals and magazines in my bookshop.

Australian studies are, of course, only a small part of the overall teaching in each university department and they have a limited budget so this partly explains their difficulties in obtaining good resources. There are some exceptions, such as Toulouse, where there is, I am told, a good library of Australian books. This is due to the work of Professor Xavier Pons and his predecessors.

Librarians tell me that, by law, they must purchase books from delegated outlets so it seems that individual academics and their students, rather than libraries, will be the likely customers of an Australian bookshop in Paris. I need to find out much more about the French universities' involvement in Australian studies as I sense that they could be very influential, both in conveying images of Australia and in dispersing Australian books. Still, this is a good beginning and, as the old teaching adage says, 'it's a good idea to proceed from the known to the unknown.'

Someone tells me that there has already been an Australian bookshop in Paris, Cannibal Pierce. The owners were Australian poet June Shenfield and Australian artist Ken Shepherd and the shop is still there, somewhere near Saint-Denis. Sadly, it has closed. I would dearly love to meet them to hear about their experiences so try to contact them – perhaps we can help each other.

For weeks I try unsuccessfully to phone the owners of Cannibal Pierce so eventually I decide to go out to see the bookshop for myself. I find it but the shutters are in place and the shop has an air of silence and loneliness. It is a long way from the centre of Paris and quite a long way from the nearest metro. People in Paris live such busy lives that I imagine distance would have been the main problem for the owners of this bookshop. I have come again to a dead end.

An Australian bookshop would need to be in a central position with lots of passing traffic. My dream of a tiny bookshop in a quiet corner of Paris recedes further into the distance. A central position will be a major priority.

Chapter 6

A LONDON INTERLUDE AND A FRENCH HOMECOMING

'La littérature ne permet pas de marcher, mais elle permet de respirer.'

'Literature doesn't make walking possible, but it makes breathing possible.'

Roland Barthes

LONDON, 1994

Towards the end of my market research stay in France I visit London for a few days because in my Big Red Book there is a note about an Australian bookshop in London. I decide to go by train and ferry. This is convenient and also means that I will see a lot of the countryside, both in the north of France and in England.

I spend three very pleasant days with my favourite niece, Catherine, and her husband, Wade. They are living on Richmond Hill, close to the Thames, and the view from the top of the hill of cattle grazing on pasture is unexpectedly rural and very peaceful. The walk along the river is leisurely and full of interest. We come upon a small second-hand bookstall where I find a copy of the English edition of Beth Yahp's book *Crocodile Fury*. I also explore central London and am surprised to find the underground railway much smaller and less efficient than the Paris metro. The traffic jams are irritating and make it difficult to gauge how much time you need to move from one place to another. There and then I decide that getting around in Paris is much easier than in London.

I visit many bookshops but Foyles particularly entrances me, despite the glamour of some of the newer book emporiums. Because it seems more higgledy-piggledy than the others, I have the feeling that it might be possible to find almost any book there if you searched long enough. The books don't appear to be catalogued – it's a case of 'seek and ye shall find' – but I love this kind of bookshop.

From the phone directory I find an address for the Australian bookshop in London but when I arrive there, the shop is empty. I go to a nearby shop and ask whether they can tell me anything about it. They tell me that some of the stock is in the basement of another bookshop, not far away. I talk with the owner of that shop and he tells me that Jim Hunt, who owns the Australian bookshop, has been ill. He takes me downstairs where I look at some of the books, still packed away in cardboard boxes. They seem to be an interesting cross-section of second-hand Australian books but there's not much I can do as there seems to be no way of contacting Mr Hunt. Again I have come to a dead end. I would have loved to talk with Jim Hunt but instead I'll try writing to him when I am back in Australia.

On the ferry going back to France, the Kent Fire Brigade treats us to the spectacle of a fire drill, which, while fun and certainly necessary, results in our late arrival in Calais. I miss my train connection, which should have delivered me to Paris in daylight hours. The trip home becomes complicated and distressing when towards midnight I am robbed at the Gare du Nord in Paris, where three men encircle me and offer their help as I'm standing at the ticket machine.

I tell them to go away and they shuffle backwards. I try to watch them as I buy my ticket and replace my wallet in my handbag but five minutes later I realise that the wallet is gone. How they did it I can't imagine, but I am shattered when I think of all that needs to be done to replace the wallet and its contents.

I have met people who dislike cities in which they have been robbed or had some other bad experience but I don't feel any particular resentment towards Paris, possibly because the first time my wallet was stolen was in the up-market suburb of Double Bay in Sydney. But my spirits sink even lower when I reach my apartment to find the gas has been turned off and I can have neither the longed-for bath nor a cup of tea.

I am pleased to discover that returning to France from England gives me a feeling of homecoming. In a way, this is strange because during my childhood my father still talked of England as the mother country and greatly revered the Queen and the royal family. Considering the final part of the journey back to Paris, it is just as well that I feel this way. I am exhausted and cold but it still seems like home.

The next day my neighbours tell me that during the weekend they thought they could smell gas coming from my apartment and that indeed I am very lucky because last time this happened the *pompiers* (firemen who do all sorts of rescue jobs) had to break the window above the front door to gain access to the apartment. I don't think there was really any leakage this time but people apparently become a bit nervous in these old buildings and I'm told that a gas leakage is not unusual.

They tell me that in a few years' time most of the gas and electricity meters will be updated and the gas pipelines checked and changed to natural gas. I hope they will also do something about the frightening power points which come loose at the wall over time because there is no switch to turn them off – you simply pull out the appliance. If it's a tight fit, the power point moves outwards until sometimes it is just hanging there. Today, when I phone the Gas Department they tell me a tradesman *could* come but if I want to I can turn the gas back on with the aid of the back of a teaspoon, so this I do. *Vive la France!* I'm learning how to deal calmly with the inescapable details of everyday life and hopefully it will stand me in good stead in future years.

Despite all the dead ends, French friends and acquaintances have been very encouraging about my bookshop idea. By the end of my stay, I have met so many Parisians and discovered many like-minded people who have become close friends and supporters. I believe that, with hard work, the proposed Australian bookshop could be successful. I do not deceive myself into thinking that a small bookshop will ever earn a fortune, but I decide that I am prepared to support it for five years until it begins to make a small profit.

I am more convinced than ever of the need to nurture and promote travelling Australian artists so that they become an accepted part of the international arts scene and I believe that the establishment of an independent bookshop, which will hopefully become an integral part of the Parisian arts community, is one way of achieving this goal.

Chapter 7

THE DOSSIER

'[Elaine] just charmed the socks off the French literati and it was delicious to watch. I'll never forget her warmth or her generosity – she was a wonderfully motherly presence as I was finding my feet amongst the fierce black polonecks of the French literary scene.'

Nikki Gemmell

MELBOURNE, 1994

The twenty-four-hour-long flight between Australia and Europe, with no stopover, is a test of endurance for most people and I am no exception. When I travelled to Europe in 1987, my back was so painful that I lay spread-eagled on the floor when I spent half an hour in the transit lounge of a very grubby Indian airport. I didn't care who saw me – I just wanted relief from the pain and simply closed my eyes and ignored those who walked around or stepped over me. This return flight is much more pleasant as my head is buzzing with ideas and plans and I have now learnt that if I sit bolt upright for the whole flight my back hurts less.

I'm heading for Melbourne because the tenants are still occupying my Sydney house and my daughter, Ginny, has invited me to stay with her until they leave. As I rarely sleep on planes there is plenty of time for reflection and planning. My seven-month sojourn in Paris has provided me with a network of friends I know will support me if and when I decide to go ahead and create an Australian bookshop. There is Nicole, always so vivacious and lively, who has taught me much about French attitudes to the *patrimoine* (the cultural icons); Alan and Gordon, with whom I share many interests, especially food, wine and music; Barbara and her French helpers from the Sydney Coffee Shop, who have explained many of the essential steps needed in order to establish a business in France; Jacques and Vivienne, who have introduced me to many of the finer details of daily life in Paris; Valerie and Sandra, with whom I've shared many new cultural experiences and, of course, my son, David, whose network of friends has made me feel that I am among a kind of French family.

Having decided that I can live alone in Paris with this great team of friends to back me up, I begin to examine aspects of the market research I have just completed. Although I had no luck with the representatives of the Australia France Foundation and the first of the French–Australian groups, every other French person I've interviewed has expressed interest and promised support. Just before I left I made contact with the new Cultural Officer at the Australian Embassy and, although she was unable to give me any advice, she was, at least, friendly and willing to help, should my dream materialise.

During my Big Red Book days I found an address in a French Government magazine and wrote to La centre de documentation at the Services de l'administration centrale in rue Saint-Honoré, which is administered by the Ministry of Culture in Paris. They are in charge of all laws relating to books and to reading and sent me a bundle of papers under the title *Direction du livre et de la lecture*. These papers contained information regarding *le loi du livre* (laws related to the buying and selling of books in France) and I studied them carefully. A couple of the laws may need clarifying but I will deal with this when the need arises. While living in Avenue Parmentier I discovered that in Paris there are many more institutions devoted to culture and, more specifically, books, so I will explore them all if and when I am granted a long-term visa.

There are more than thirty universities in France teaching some kind of Australian studies and it seems that the teachers and students will be pleased to have an Australian bookshop in Paris, and gather from reading the *loi du livre* that most libraries aren't able to buy directly from a small independent bookshop as they are compelled by law to buy from specified distributors if they spend over a certain amount of money. Another problem is that University libraries may take six months to pay for books purchased because all large accounts must be processed through a central system. I am gradually learning the realities of France's centralised administration, which dates back to the days of Napoleon.

I found no bookshop in Paris selling Australian books alongside their French translations and believe that doing this, along with encouraging more translations of Australian books, will play an important part in the success or otherwise of the bookshop. There seem to be many translators interested in Australian books and I believe that the general public will also be interested, once the bookshop is established as part of the Parisian community and effective marketing takes place.

Apart from an occasional book launch at the Australian Embassy and at the Village Voice Bookshop, there is no regular venue for Australian writers and artists visiting Paris, yet almost every other country in the world seems to have a cultural centre here, usually including a bookshop and tourism office. In a city like Paris, where all the cultures of the world pass through, it seems short-sighted to me that Australia is represented only by bureaucracy and that it is left to the French themselves to try to present Australia's creative and intellectual ideas, as well as its tourist attractions. We certainly seem to have an island mentality. Are we afraid to talk with strangers? Our artists and writers should be represented in all the major cities of Europe and Asia, not to mention the rest of the world. Lofty ideas, perhaps, but I believe that each of us can make a difference.

Before I left Paris, Barbara from the Sydney Coffee Shop suggested I go to the French Consulate in Australia as soon as possible after my return in order to apply for a long-term visa. If granted, the long-term visa would lead to a ten-year visa, a *carte de séjour* (residency card) and a *carte de commerçante* (business permit). She told me that she was able to do all the preliminary work in Australia herself, thus saving a lot of money. I decide to begin with a visit to the French Consulate in Melbourne.

Barbara also gave me an important contact at the French Chambre de Commerce in Paris. He has been a great help to her and she recommended that I send him my business plan as soon as it is completed.

By now I have convinced myself that I should go ahead with my plan and can't wait for the plane to reach Australia so that I can begin.

⚜ ⚜

Full of energy and enthusiasm, I'm back in Melbourne, ready to start immediately. My daughter and her husband are encouraging and excited about my plans. They understand because they too are book lovers. They suggest that I might like to gain more sales experience by working with their friend Ross Reading of Greens Environmental Bookshop in Flinders Lane.

I begin working for Ross, a colourful Melbourne identity who, with his then wife, Dorothy, opened the original Readings bookshop in Carlton in 1968. He is a kind, gentle man but can be a hard taskmaster and I'm sure he thinks that a woman of a certain age shouldn't be running across to the other side of the world opening bookshops. He says one day that he doesn't see why I want to leave Melbourne when

I have grandchildren living here. My daughter is present and she says, 'Ross, she can't just sit there and watch them grow!'

In a way, she has summarised my feelings in a nutshell. I adore my family and they are the most important thing in my life but I've always wanted them to be independent and they are. They all lead exceptionally busy lives so I need to be busy as well to avoid feeling lonely. I have friends who don't work and their lives are full but, unlike them, I seem to need a project to keep me engaged and fulfilled. It's probably a matter of upbringing – I grew up in a small country town where everyone knew everyone and people helped each other and participated in communal activities, so I'm happiest when I'm involved with people in general as well as in particular.

While I'm working at Greens, Ross devises all kinds of tasks to put me off my dream and sometimes, at the end of the day, I am so tired and in such pain that I feel like weeping. I can't complain, because Ross might think me not fit enough for the job. Some of the work is heavy, but I do it and after several months he sees how determined I am to open my bookshop in Paris. After that he takes great pains to involve me in all the normal retail bookselling operations.

He teaches me to reconcile accounts, do the daily banking, order books, return books to publishers, process mail-orders, arrange window-displays and in-store displays, and operate the computerised bibliographic database. Sometimes Ross leaves me in sole charge of the shop for up to a week at a time and, when I ask him for a reference, he writes that he has come to have complete confidence in my abilities to operate a specialist bookshop and comments that I show considerable flair in dealing with the public. Like most people, this is the part of the job I love most and I meet many charming and interesting Melbourne booklovers during this period. At Da Capo in Sydney I also loved selling and dealing with the public. When people are united by a common love of books, the transaction between salesperson and customer can become one of life's more memorable experiences, perhaps not in large bookshops but certainly in the smaller, independent bookshops.

During this period I spend a lot of time attending a physiotherapist and I sometimes doubt the wisdom of purusing my bookshop dream. In the end I decide that, if I'm going to endure pain for the rest of my life, I might as well be doing something useful as opposed to sitting around feeling miserable, so I push myself along.

At Ross's suggestion I become an associate member of the Australian Booksellers' Association (ABA) and put together a business plan based on their guidelines and also from information obtained from the Victorian Small Business Advisory Service. I decide to name the shop the Australian Bookshop and determine that its aim will be to sell both new and second-hand Australian books, in English and in French, and to support and promote Australian artists who visit Paris.

I send this business plan to my contact at the Paris Chamber of Commerce and am thrilled to receive from him a letter of approval, which will be most helpful when I visit the French Consulate in Melbourne. I can't wait to say that I want to open a bookshop in Paris and flourish my letter of support from the French Chamber of Commerce. I am elated!

This letter is, at present, the only official written offer of support for an Australian bookshop in Paris. The Chamber of Commerce representative has received my business plan, from which it is clear that a profit cannot be expected in the first three years, but that the business should then break even and after that, it will definitely make a small profit each year. This is normal for small bookshops, which aren't a way to make lots of money. At this stage of my life I live alone, have experienced a very satisfying career in teaching and have no financial dependants. Because of this, and because I believe that the promotion of Australian writing is essential if we are to participate in international dialogue, I am prepared to live simply in France and to support the bookshop in a philanthropic way. My three adult children have encouraged me and given me their full support and, now, receiving this letter of support from Paris, I feel that I have the strength to forge ahead.

My next step is to visit the office of the French Consul in Melbourne, where, discouragingly, I am told in a very charming way that, despite my letter of approval, what I want to do is very difficult and that it could possibly take more than a year to complete the business dossier and have it approved, even if the application is prepared by a lawyer.

I tell the Consul's representative that I will do it myself to save the expense, so she gives me a pile of forms to fill in, including an application for a ten-year visa (*un visa de longue durée*) and a long list of documents I must obtain. Every document pertaining to my life must be found, translated by an accredited translator and witnessed by a lawyer accredited by the French authorities. Birth and divorce certificates, health and insurance statements, educational and business qualifications, financial background, bank statements, title deeds of the house, references – there seems no end to it but I am optimistic and begin the task quite cheerfully.

I decide to treat it as a challenge and approach it step by step. This is not as easy as I hoped it would be: for instance, I cannot apply for a business permit if I don't have a business address in France but I can't have a business address in France if I don't have a *carte de commerçant*. Fortunately David has told me that there is usually a solution to these kinds of French laws and we discover that I can pay for a temporary office address to use while preparing the dossier.

By May 1995 I am becoming irritated at the delays. I have to visit the French Consulate's accredited doctor, who cannot immediately give me a satisfactory medical certificate because he thinks that the scar on my lung might indicate tuberculosis. In vain I protest that the scar has been checked by Sydney specialists who decided that it was a scar from severe bronchitis I experienced as a child. But this 'official' doctor won't listen to me and says that I must supply a letter from a specialist confirming that the Sydney tests were clear. The paperwork seems unending.

The health form also requests that I be tested for syphilis. I begin to wonder just how old these forms are and I suggest to the accredited lawyer that I might do better in Sydney where they surely must process a lot of business applications in a more streamlined fashion.

'You can't do that,' he says, 'the dossier must be prepared in your home state.'

'New South Wales is my home state,' I say. 'At the moment, Melbourne is my temporary address, but my permanent dwelling is in Sydney.'

The Paddington tenants are moving out in early June so off I go to Sydney where things move very quickly thanks to the efficiency of the much bigger and more experienced French Consulate in Market Street. I no longer have to pay a lawyer to witness documents because I am told that an alternative is to swear an affidavit (*attestation*) before a

77

Justice of the Peace. With the help of the very capable woman in charge of business applications the dossier is quickly completed and sent off to the Préfecture de Police in Paris. She tells me to go ahead with my plans as everything is in order. She also tells me that if I had had a million dollars to spend on the business, I would have escaped preparation of the dreaded dossier.

I begin a business language course at the French Chamber of Commerce in Sydney and, although I have started late, it's very useful and enjoyable. The teacher, Odile, is excellent and there is an interesting mixture of students including several lawyers and an architect. At the end, Odile tells me that I have made good progress but that it might still be a good idea to ask someone to check my business letters. There are so many conventions to remember that I decide that I must look for a book of pro forma examples.

After an announcement by the Australian Government that they intend to support small businesses, I wonder whether this applies to small export businesses or small Australian businesses in other countries as well as those in Australia. It's not clear so I contact Austrade and meet some very kind people who give willingly of their time. The gentleman who visits me is very interested in my project and tells me that he thinks someone in Canberra *once* supported the export of Australian books.

This is a bit ominous and finally it becomes clear that the old rule that hindered me previously still applies: Austrade cannot help me unless I decide to spend AU$30,000 on advertising in the first year. So much for helping small businesses. I think this unreasonable as I am sure that because of my past experience and my contacts I can do the marketing and publicity without spending this amount.

In my Big Red Book I have already listed the books I want for the opening stock so my next task is to write to the Australian publishers and arrange interviews. The books are chosen partly from my observation of sales at Greens and partly from my attempts to gauge which books will suit the French market. For example, I think the general French reader will not understand certain kinds of Australian humour, with its heavy, Anglo-Saxon irony. I know that the French are already interested in Australian Indigenous art and culture and they are also familiar with some Australian films. To these I add the standard classic Australian novels, the works of some emerging writers, some general non-fiction works and some of our best children's books. I have a special interest in music, theatre, food and travel writing, so examples of these books have also been added to my Big Red Book.

From these lists I choose the appropriate publishing companies, meet their overseas marketing representatives and finalise the orders with them, noting also their suggestions. Without exception, they are friendly, enthusiastic and helpful. It is necessary for me to approach each publisher individually because, at this time, most Australian distributors do not send books overseas. Some Australian publishers use distributors or publishing firms in the UK and insist that I must order from them, because of territorial rights, but most agree to supply me by sending the books to my shipping agent in Melbourne who will consolidate them and send them to France where they will be received, processed and delivered by another shipping agent.

Consolidation, shipping and delivery costs are high and added to this are customs and TVA – a tax similar to the GST, except the French Government has a more enlightened view of the importance of culture so books attract only 5.5 per cent TVA whereas many other goods and services attract 20.6 per cent TVA I must admit to feeling a bit nervous in view of the high costs involved but I hope that customers will be willing to pay more for products that have limited availability.

At the 1995 Australian Booksellers' Association conference in July I meet some booksellers who tell me about their colleague and friend, Glenda Stewart, who loves books and loves France. Eventually I meet her and she is just as they have described – a warm, friendly person who loves bookselling and has made a special study of children's books. Her response to my plan is overwhelmingly enthusiastic. She says, 'Great! I'll be able to help you because we will be in France for six months in 1996.'

I can't believe my good fortune and promise to keep her in touch with developments after I reach Paris. The ABA conference is also helpful in practical ways as there are sessions on all aspects of book-selling. I spend a lot of time with another friendly bookseller from Katherine in the Northern Territory – it's a long way from Katherine to Paris but the web of Australian Bookshop connections is already establishing itself.

As I make my preparations to depart I begin to talk excitedly about my plans and soon find that my world is divided into two kinds of people – those who understand and those who do not. I go to a reading at Gleebooks where I meet an Australian author and his wife. Their responses to my proposed adventure are typical of the general reactions. The author says, 'Oh, that's wonderful. How exciting!'

His wife says, 'Why on earth would you want to do that? And why in France?'

Some people will never understand why anyone would do something for little or no financial gain, but, as I have seldom made a decision for financial reasons, I find it difficult to see why they can't understand. Happily for me there are also people who say, 'How wonderful – I wish I could go with you.'

A few of my close friends seem annoyed with me – it's as though they think that at sixty years of age you should just behave nicely and have a few hobbies to keep you busy when you aren't babysitting the grandchildren. The fact that I don't want to do this is in no way a criticism of my friends. I simply don't want to retire.

I feel a little chastened when an acquaintance says, 'Oh, I told my daughter how much I envy you. I would love to have a bookshop in Paris but my daughter said, "Oh no, Mum, you wouldn't do that because you couldn't bring yourself to leave your children and grandchildren."'

Finally the groundwork seems to be complete so I negotiate with a removalist and begin to pack the possessions I want to take to France with me and organise the renting of my house. I visit my family in Melbourne and they all say they will come to Paris during the next year so it's not too difficult leaving them. Once my possessions are on the sea I will have to move quickly because I must find a destination for them in France. It's very exciting but not a little terrifying.

My back is very painful so a rheumatologist at St Vincent's Hospital gives me some cortisone injections to help me with the plane journey and the first few busy weeks in Paris. A week before leaving Australia I sell my car and then the countdown begins until, thanks to the help of friends, I am at the airport saying goodbye to Sydney and what has been an eventful twelve years. It's always sad to leave, but the world has become so much smaller now that it's mostly '*au revoir*', and seldom really 'goodbye'. Everyone promises to visit me in Paris and soon I'm on my way.

Chapter 8

IN SEARCH OF A SHOP

'Wandering re-establishes the original harmony which once existed
between man and the universe.'

Anatole France

PARIS, 1995

Paris in her winter guise is familiar to me and Christmas decorations are already in place when I arrive there at the end of 1995. I am accustomed to being there during our long school holidays, the Australian summer, and have grown to love the preparations leading up to the winter festive season, from the lavish decorations at the big department stores like Galeries Lafayettes and Printemps to the more intense than usual concentration upon the food and wine which will accompany *le Réveillon*, the traditional feast on Christmas Eve. Not for nothing is gastronomy referred to by the French as the 'Eighth Art'.

Shortly after my arrival in Paris I receive a letter from Madame Danielle Potel-Doyle, the French Vice-Consul in Sydney, saying that that my papers have been approved by the Préfecture de Police (the main Police Department, which is situated on the Île de la Cité), that I have been granted a ten-year visa and that I will receive my *visa de long séjour* and my *carte de commerçant* when I report to the Paris Préfecture with my papers. Although I have applied for a ten-year visa, the Australian Bookshop is, for me, a five-year plan: I will support it financially for five years and then review it. The letter from Madame Potel-Doyle is like a late Christmas present and I feel a great sense of achievement at having successfully completed the dreaded dossier in less than a year.

The letter tells me that I must make an appointment with the Préfecture as soon as possible after my arrival in France. To do so takes endless phone calls but I finally receive a notice assigning me a rendezvous at the Préfecture on 29 January 1996 at 9 am, *Escalier E, 1er étage* (staircase E, first floor). I am told to bring my passport, my ten-year visa and proof of address plus 680FF for stamp taxes.

The day arrives and I set off in a cheerful frame of mind. The Préfecture is a huge building, built around a central square, opposite the imposing Palais de Justice and the jewel-like Sainte Chapelle, but definitely lacking the charms of these two buildings, which are much visited by tourists. I am not bothered by the long queue I see snaking around the back because French friends have forewarned me: the building also processes immigration. I eventually pass through the entrance hall with its guards and X-ray machine and am directed to the right, up a wide marble staircase that leads to a long corridor with settees like church pews on either side. There are signs on the doorways facing onto the corridor and, after perusing them all, I decide on one that seems applicable to my situation and sit down to wait. I have a piece of paper in my hand indicating that I have an appointment at the Préfecture at 9 am, so there I sit, awaiting my call.

Time passes and my name is not called. Many other names *are* called and their owners disappear behind various doors; after an hour has passed, there is a much smaller group of people sitting along the corridor, all looking even more nervous than I am now feeling. My optimism has worn thin. Some of the others seem to have their lawyers with them and there is a great deal of tension in the air. I think of Kafka. Finally, at about ten o'clock, I summon up the courage to knock on the door and enter a long room which is even more intimidating than the corridor outside: lining one of the longer walls and taking up more than half of the room is a row of rough wooden booths, a bit like polling-booths in Australia, but with a chair in each. I am told to sit in the first of these booths.

'What do you want?' asks a woman behind the counter of the booth.

'*S'il vous plaît, madame*, I have an appointment for 9 am.'

'What is your name?'

'Madame Lewis.'

'Wait outside.'

From this I deduce that I have done the right thing – if I hadn't entered the office to give them my name I might have waited all day for an interview, yet there is no sign anywhere instructing people to report inside. As I wait, I wonder how many others sit waiting for hours before they become aware of the procedure by some sort of osmosis.

I will return to the Préfecture many times and there is never any clarification of the process. Now I understand why so many migrants bring their lawyers with them but I don't want to pay legal fees on top of all the other charges I know await me so I sit there alone. The atmosphere is tense and no one smiles.

When my name is finally called I sit down in one of the booths and wait for ages until someone comes. I hand over my dossier, feeling pleased that it is so complete. There is silence for what seems an eternity while the policewoman peruses my papers. She then begins to tell me all the things that are missing. I protest that I have provided everything on the list given to me by her country's representatives in Australia and that the French Government has already approved the ten-year visa.

She becomes angry. 'That doesn't matter,' she says, 'I need this and this and this . . .'

It's all too much for me, after a year of meticulous preparations, and I am so disappointed that I burst into tears, which is about the worst thing I could do because she looks at me scornfully, ushers me out and calls in the next person. Rule number one: when dealing with French bureaucracy do not burst into tears.

When I arrive back at David's apartment he is surprised that I found the experience so daunting and offers to go back the next day to clarify matters. I don't know precisely what happens during his interview, but when he returns home he tells me that he quite understands why I wept. It was frustrating even for him, and he is accustomed to dealing with French authorities. He says that while he was waiting a Russian couple was trying to obtain permission to bring an elderly parent to Paris. They had plenty of money to look after her, but still their application was refused and when they protested the official became angry and raised her voice.

I am reminded of a book I read in 1994, *The Narrow Street*, written by Paul Elliot. First published in 1942, it has a wonderful description of life in rue de la Huchette between the two World Wars. Rue de la Huchette is a narrow little street that runs parallel to the Seine, off Boulevard Saint-Michel, just a few yards from the quai. Elliot writes that centuries ago, when Saint-Germain-des-Prés was a cow paddock, the first Parisians left their fortified island in the middle of the Seine and settled in this street. In the 1920s and '30s it was still a village with little shops including a butcher, grocer, delicatessen, dairy and – Elliot's favourite spot – the Hôtel du Caveau, with its wonderful mediaeval cellar. Most of the buildings are still there but today the street has become one of those unpleasant areas where waiters stand spruiking in front of cafés and restaurants, competing with one another in an effort to lure tourists into their establishments.

Elliot lived in the 'narrow street' for many years and he wrote lovingly of the other people who lived there during that time. One of these was Hortense Berthelot, described as a clerk at the Préfecture, and another was '*Le Navet*', a *petit fonctionnaire* (minor civil servant) who also worked at the Préfecture. Elliot describes them vividly and goes on to comment in general:

'One cannot exaggerate the inefficiency of a French public office, especially those to which members of the public were forced, all too often, to present themselves for heckling and abuse.'

He adds, later on in the book: 'renewals of permission to stay in France were sometimes granted, after months or years of delay, with a rubber stamp.'

Plus ça change! Fifty years later, nothing has changed and I eventually receive my rubber stamp. This disdainful treatment is not reserved for foreigners; a French friend, Anne, tells me that she is always asked to go away and find another document, no matter how hard she tries to cover all contingencies. According to her, mastering French bureaucracy is difficult for the French as well, but if you are a foreigner you have the feeling that you are being singled out for maltreatment.

My experience at the Préfecture was humorous, in retro-spect, but very time-consuming and annoying while it was happening. Because of the large population in Paris things always move slowly and you need to set aside at least half a day for one small task and be prepared to go away and come back on another day. I learn never to show that I am upset but to appear firm, demanding and determined. Gradually I develop my own *modus operandi*, which is to write down everything I am told, present it to the official and ask, in a very stern voice, *'Est-ce que j'ai bien compris?'* ('Have I understood you correctly?'). After that, I receive their full attention and the matter is usually resolved without delay.

⁂

In early February 1996, I am still staying with David and his partner, Belle, at 47 rue de Douai, not far from Place de Clichy. The apartment is small and I am occupying the tiny second bedroom which David uses as a study. I am conscious of the fact that he usually composes at the desk, which is now littered with my papers. As well as the main bedroom, there is a lounge/dining room and a very small kitchen – not really sufficient space for three adults. David and Belle are at the beginning of both their personal and musical relationship and their new group, Paris Combo, is in the process of being created, so I try to creep out early in the mornings without disturbing them and return as late as possible in order to give them some space.

The tourist strip between Clichy, Blanche and Pigalle is not particularly attractive these days because of all the large buses which pull in there each day and night to visit the peep-shows and other erotica, but you only have to walk a couple of blocks down a side street to find the village life of Place de Clichy. I love getting to know yet another quartier and appreciate particularly the oysters at Brasserie Wepler, which is more than 100 years old. It claims to have been the first oyster-seller in Paris and freshly opened oysters are still its speciality, as well as many other varieties of delicious seafood. In earlier days the brasserie was a café-restaurant with billiards, shows and dancing and was a meeting place for great names like Picasso, Utrillo, Modigliani, Henry Miller, Truffaut and Chabrol. Today it is typical of many of the grand old brasseries with its red and gold awnings and its Belle Epoque ambience.

Further across, close to Métro Les Abbesses in rue Yvonne Le Tac is a wonderful smaller bookshop, Librairie des Abbesses. The owner of this bookshop is an enterprising and dedicated bookseller, Marie-Rose Guarniéri, and I call in frequently to see what she is doing. I also become very familiar with the BNP (Banque Nationale de Paris) at Place Clichy because I am waiting for money to be transferred into my business account, which is registered there. I know that the money has left Australia to be forwarded to the B.N.P. via Barclay's. It seems to have been lost in transit because every time I go to the bank the woman in charge says she is following the case. When, after several weeks,

I insist that urgent action is needed, she seems to become annoyed and says indignantly, '*Madame, je m'occupe de vous!*' (I'm looking after you!) She suggests that perhaps the intermediary bank has not forwarded it.

I decide to take action myself because it is a large sum of money that is, apparently, floating through the ether. At Barclay's I ascertain that indeed the money has been received and sent on to the French bank. I obtain the number of the transaction and return to Clichy. Even with this evidence it still takes many more weeks for them to trace my money and the whole experience is stressful.

Part of the problem, I suppose, is that, despite my brief attendance at the French Chamber of Commerce's excellent business language course in Sydney, I am not accustomed to using French business vocabulary. For example, when Madame at the bank asks me for my *K. bis*, I think I hear '*cabisse*' and say, 'I'm afraid I don't know that word. What does it mean?'

She explains that it is simply the business certificate issued by the Chamber of Commerce, generally referred to as *K.(b)*. There are a lot of such acronyms to memorise and I am on a swift learning curve. It does occur to me that perhaps my money is being used by the bank for short-term investment purposes but I think it prudent to say nothing. On the other hand, the Government probably still processes money through a central system, according to the

Napoleonic code. As yet, the use of computers doesn't seem to have lessened the masses of paperwork used to finally complete this transaction.

There is much more to explore in the quartier around Clichy but now that the Préfecture has endorsed my papers, I must begin walking the streets to search for a shop. At first I spend a lot of time wandering around the Bastille area, near the cellar where I was first inspired, but eventually I come to the conclusion that this area is not really suitable for the Australian Bookshop because it has now developed into a buzzing night district, containing many bars and clubs as well as the new Opéra. People seem to go to Bastille to eat, drink and be entertained. There's nothing wrong with that, but it is not an atmosphere that leads to buying books, unless you happen to have a bar combined with a bookshop, like the enviable and beautiful *librairie* (bookshop) in the Marais, La Belle Hortense. *Pas possible!* I decide that I must go south, cross the Seine and begin walking around the Left Bank and its environs, the traditional home of French publishing. This is a long way from rue de Douai so I need to find accommodation as well as a shop.

I am walking the streets because French friends have told me that many people with businesses for sale and rooms to rent do not advertise in the newspapers. They also advise me that it could take six months to find a shop so once again patience is required. I approach some real estate agents and gradually build up a network of Parisians who know that I am searching for a shop. The accommodation problem is more difficult because I'm not sure where I'll be working so, to save money, I stay for a while in small, cheap hotels in the northern part of Paris. (I can't afford the hotels on the Left Bank and it's comforting to be close to my Paris family, even though they aren't always available.) These little hotels are clean and well run but very impersonal and at the end of a day of fruitless searching it is sad to return to one of these bland establishments, which seem to be run by faceless people.

To my alarm, the army of friends I met in 1994 is gradually diminishing in numbers. It seems almost unbelievable that the most Parisian of them all, Nicole, has fallen in love with an Englishman and gone to live in Brighton. Alan and Gordon have moved to Munich — it's not far away and they have promised to return to Paris as often as possible, but they still aren't here. Sandra is in Rome and won't be returning to Paris for at least a year, while Valerie has also fallen in love and returned to the U.S.

Jacques is still here and he is extremely helpful, allowing me to use his office and his computer while my search continues. He is a wonderful listener and is interested in my plans, introducing me to people and advising me on the endless minutiae of daily life in a big city. Unfortunately, problems arise with our friendship because although he and

Vivienne both told me in 1994 that they had an open marriage, her behaviour now that I am back in Paris indicates that she is not happy for Jacques to see me too frequently.

Barbara and the Sydney Coffee Shop have disappeared with no forwarding address. The Australian Embassy library has closed and the librarian, Loretta, has also disappeared. The two French businesswomen I met through Barbara are still around but I am uncertain about their agenda. I am in a temporary slump and have to push myself to keep going. When I begin to feel like a character from one of Jean Rhys' Parisian novels I realise it is time to move out of the third cheap hotel and find more cheerful accommodation.

A friend of a friend offers me a room with shared use of her kitchen and bathroom. It's 3000 francs a month, which seems quite expensive, but because it is recommended by a friend and is situated in a beautiful building on Boulevard Raspail, I accept the offer. At last I am living on the Left Bank – Boulevard Raspail borders the Latin Quarter, between Saint-Germain-des-Prés and Montparnasse, and is regarded as a prestigious address. The building I live in is impressively elegant with its grand marble foyer, large apartments and quiet atmosphere. Each day I pass the flamboyantly Art Deco Hotel Lutètia; built during the Belle Epoque, it dominates the intersection of rue de Sèvres and Boulevard Raspail and faces the Eiffel Tower. It must be the most palatial building on the Left Bank – many French friends tell me it was commandeered by the Germans during the World War II occupation and became the Gestapo headquarters in Paris. Since then it has been redecorated and is, I'm told, just as spectacular on the inside, being filled with ornate Art Deco objects, flamboyant stair-cases and glistening crystal chandeliers.

I gather that my landlady usually rents her spare room to American tourists and, as she does not speak English, these are purely business transactions and little communication ensues. We speak briefly in the kitchen, where I am allo-cated a third of a shelf in the refrigerator, but other than that she has little to say to me.

I am disappointed as I had hoped for more of a cultural exchange. I am busy all day but when I come home in the evening I must pass through her enormous living/dining area to reach my room and then back again to use the kitchen. This is not too uncomfortable if she is sitting watching television but when she has dinner parties I feel embarrassed at having to pass her guests in order to enter my room, return to the kitchen and then go back to my room to sit and eat my meal alone. I stay out as late as I can, especially at weekends, but I soon begin to feel exhausted because I am walking all day, either searching for a shop, making business contacts or completing the necessary administration.

By chance I discover an advertisement in *FUSAC* (an American expats' magazine) which sounds interesting – it is for an apartment at Pernety, behind Montparnasse, and the family are going away for *les grandes vacances* (the long holidays) so want someone to look after their home. *Les grandes vacances* can last for the whole of July and August, and this turns out to be the case with the owner of this apartment, Aurore.

So I move to a more bohemian quartier where I am very happy. I can come and go as I wish and soon begin to feel less tired. When the family returns from their holidays, I stay on for a while at their invitation. They are atypically open to sharing their house and invite me to eat meals with them and attend family parties. Aurore is a beautiful woman who has been an artists' model, which explains the many semi-nude portraits of her hanging on the walls of the apartment. She loves to chat and we spend a lot of time discussing family matters and love affairs as well as art and books and life in general. I am immensely grateful to her but I know that when her son comes home I will have to move on, yet again.

Alongside this complicated saga of personal accommodation problems, my days are fully occupied with viewing shops and making business contacts. During the day I'm able to live outside myself and focus on the opening of the bookshop. Of course I enjoy my own pleasures but over the years I have learnt that it's possible to derive happiness from focusing on projects outside the self. It's a question of survival.

In the evenings I sometimes go to concerts or the theatre with Belle and David and am delighted to be able to attend their first Paris Combo gig in May. They play for four nights and are enthusiastically received. As a mother, I am proud and happy to be with them at the beginning of their success. I also meet Belle's parents, Françoise and Robert, who are warm, friendly country people from Berry Bouy, a small town in Central France.

I look at many shops alone and an agent shows me more, but a lot of them are dingy and situated in out-of-the-way little streets. I see some of the more dismal streets of Paris and begin to despair of ever finding something pleasant and affordable. I admit to myself that I don't want to spend every day in a grungy back lane.

While exploring the Mouffetard area, in the 5th arrondissement, I see a 'To let' sign in the window of an attractive gift shop. I love *La Mouffe*, as rue Mouffetard is known – it is one of Paris' oldest streets and was once part of the road between Paris and Lyon. It is still a cobbled street, although the stones of the old Roman road are buried several metres below the more modern stones of today. Despite the many tourists it still has a village atmosphere, especially on market days, with vendors hawking their wares and strolling musicians adding to the atmosphere. The

Mouffetard attracts visitors and tourists and lots of local students but people rarely detour from the main strip. The shop I like is in a side street running off *La Mouffe* and I wonder whether many people would pass by this quiet square with its lovely plane tree.

I am very tempted by this pretty little shop and its pleasant outlook, so even though it is isolated I don't immediately cross it off my list. The owner is friendly and I visit her shop several times to talk with her but eventually decide that it is too far off the beaten track to be viable. Also, because it is not a bookshop, the *bail* (lease) would have to be changed. This could be expensive and would give the owner the right to raise the rent. I realise that one of the problems is that I had envisaged a small shop in a quiet street, but I have now been persuaded that if I want to sell books I must look for a good position in an area frequented by book lovers. So on I trudge.

೧௸ ௸ఌ

Other people's experiences also confirm the need to be in a central position, preferably on a tourist track, even if it means allocating more for rent than I had originally intended. The sum allocated in my business plan is equivalent to what I would pay in Melbourne so I decide to go to the upper limit. Towards the end of April, an acquaintance tells me about a shop on the Quai des Grands Augustins, close to Saint-Michel. There is a sign in the window saying that it is available to rent. I phone the owner who makes an appointment to meet me at the shop.

My first visit to the shop is in early May and I fall in love with it. It is spring; the sun is shining on the waters of the Seine, the trees are still wearing their young green leaves and from the doorway of the shop I can see the spire of the Sainte Chapelle and the rows of blossom trees at the side of Notre Dame. Across the road the stalls of the *bouquinistes* look very much as they do in ancient postcards. I feel as though I am in the very heart of Paris.

The owner, Monsieur Vinarnic, tells me that the shop was built to serve as a bookshop in the nineteenth century but has more recently been used to sell clothing. This explains the pale pink carpet. The original shelving, some of which is still lined with worn green felt, is in place although the old glass doors have been removed and are stacked in a back room. The wooden panelling is typical of the beautiful old nineteenth-century rare-book shops along rue Jacob and rue de Seine, most of which have been beautifully restored. There are also two back rooms, one with a separate entrance to rue Séguier. The other contains a sink and cooking facilities. Between these two rooms is a bathroom lined with slightly shabby wallpaper depicting the actress Sarah Bernhardt.

The shop is a dream but the rent is at the extreme top of my range. I argue to myself that I would have to pay this amount for a similar-sized shop in Melbourne and, as I don't expect to make a profit for at least three years, I can cut corners and live very simply until the business becomes established.

Negotiations begin and M. Vinarnic is very co-operative because, he tells me, both he and the people living in the apartments above the shop would much prefer a bookshop there to the other possible businesses that have applied to rent the shop. He proudly tells me that the owners of the apartments in the building include Odette Joyeux, a much-loved Parisian actress, dancer and writer who is now in her eighties. Her actor son, Claude Brasseur, is also very popular in France and I have seen him in some excellent films and on television. His father was Pierre Brasseur, another Paris icon, who is remembered for his roles in at least eighty films, including *Les Enfants du Paradis*. I am supposed to be impressed by this, and indeed I am, because I know how highly the French regard their actors and actresses.

M. Vinarnic is a flamboyant and highly successful businessman and comments one day, *à propos* of business procedures, that he has never used his own money to make money. I don't tell him that I have no option but to use my own capital – since my husband divorced me over twenty years ago I have not been able to borrow because I have no credit rating, despite the fact that together we bought and paid off four houses. I have found that a divorced woman living and working alone in Australia is not the equal of a man in the same position.

I am grateful for the help of the two French business-women during this period and think it very altruistic of them to make themselves available. However, during one of the discussions they ask M. Vinarnic about using one of the back rooms for printing materials and publishing. As I have no intention of publishing anything, I realise that they have not given up some of the ideas for an Australian cultural magazine discussed in 1994 with Barbara and Loretta. I try to make it clear to them that I don't have sufficient capital for such a venture and that I intend to focus on the bookshop.

There are endless business meetings, one of which is at M. Vinarnic's home, the most luxurious I have yet seen in Paris. He is enthusiastic and tells me that he has chosen the Australian Bookshop as a tenant from a list of 150 applications for his boutique. At last, on the fifteenth of May, he hands me the keys and I have a home for both the books and my personal effects, which are due to arrive any day from Australia. The two back rooms are a bonus as I can put the books in one room and my belongings in the other until I have a permanent home address. To celebrate the occasion, M. Vinarnic invites me to lunch at a very superior restaurant, close by the shop.

So much has happened in such a short time that my

head is whirling, but I am very happy and excited at finding such a beautiful shop and am confident that, in five years, I will make a small profit. During these past few months I have met with the trade and cultural officials from the Embassy – Sallyanne Atkinson of Austrade, Angus MacKenzie, Cultural Attaché, and Harriet O'Malley, Cultural Officer. They can't offer practical help but indicate that they will be pleased to work with me once the bookshop is set up. Jean-Paul and Monique Delamotte, who have promoted Australian literature in France since 1977, also indicate that they will be pleased to have a 'permanent focal point' for Australian writers in the heart of Paris. Monique says that she will be happy to sit in the shop and talk about the books published by their small publishing company, La Petite Maison.

Jean-Paul and Monique Delamotte's love affair with Australia began when they decided to visit in 1974 for their honeymoon and stayed on until 1977. During their stay, Jean-Paul gave courses in the French department at the University of Newcastle and at several other universities in Melbourne and Sydney. He has told me that, in those days, French was the most taught foreign language in Australia and he was astounded at the French/Australian connections he discovered. He felt that the French Government and its people should reciprocate what he saw as a great apprecia-tion of France in Australia. He was determined to lobby the

French government and publishers and fight to forge cultural links between the two countries.

This he has done by creating several associations (including the publishing company), hosting dinner parties for Australians and renting two studios in Boulogne to house visiting Australian writers and academics, as well as lobbying the government and the media. Jean-Paul has made me an honorary member of his association ACFA and given me a list of members, most of whom seem to be Australian writers and VIPs. I can assist him by displaying the books published by La Petite Maison but, as far as the lobbying goes, I don't really understand why the French Government (or the publishers, for that matter) should be any more interested in Australia than in Finland, Zimbabwe, New Zealand, *n'importe quoi*. I won't lobby the government or the publishers; my idea is to market the books as well as I can, with the hope that the bookshop will become an established Australian meeting-place in the heart of the Paris community; that it will attract publishers, translators and readers from all walks of life who will see the books, read them and decide for themselves which ones to translate and publish. It's a different approach.

Jean-Paul tells me that his other exciting discovery in Australia during the wonderful 1970s was the French-Australian writer Paul Wenz – I haven't yet read his works but am intrigued when Wenz's nephew visits the shop during the renovations and tells me that he is not particularly interested in Australia or its writers. He has lived and worked in Argentina.

I am looking forward to meeting the academics – Xavier Pons, Jean-Claude Redonnet, Maryvonne Nedeljkovic, Denise Coussy and many others – who have also been promoting Australian literature in France for years.

One of the most significant events for me this year is the renewal of my friendship with Maria Crépeau, whom I had met several years before through mutual friends. For our first meeting in 1996, I go to her apartment in the 5th arrondissement, not far from the Arènes du Lutèce, and we talk for four hours. She is, without doubt, the most fascinating person I have met in Paris and she becomes my guide and mentor as well as a true friend. We talk about books, music and travel, and together we play piano duets. We both love music and, in her eighties, she still plays very well. I spent years training to be a pianist but she is a natural musician and plays much better than I do. She is a wonderful companion and I promise myself that after the shop is opened I will make time to visit her on my day off, to enjoy her company and to seek her advice and help at understanding the nuances of French behaviour.

Maria's friends include well-known musicians and actors, and because she has lived and worked as a writer in Paris for many years, she understands the literary world very well and can guide me through these early days when I am meeting publishers and translators for the first time. For more than fifty years she was married to Australian writer Godfrey (Geoffrey) Blunden, whom I never met because he died in 1996, not long before Maria and I were reunited. They both worked as journalists for *Time-Life* magazine during World War II, and Geoffrey was also a novelist. Of his many books, the best known is probably *Charco Harbour*, the story of Captain Cook's first voyage to the Pacific in 1768.

Together, Maria and Geoffrey published a beautiful book, *Impressionists and Impressionism*; at first glance it looks like a coffee-table book but it is much more than that, dealing in depth with the late nineteenth-century painters Manet, Monet, Degas, Renoir, Pissarro and Cézanne. It is superbly illustrated in both colour and black and white and the main text is complemented by witness accounts by painters, friends, writers and critics of the time. Because of these personal comments, *Impressionists and Impressionism* is unique and I'm told it is as important today as when it was first published. Maria and Geoffrey both lived long and interesting lives and Maria has so many amazing stories to tell that she is a delight to be with. Without her practical support and friendship, I don't think I would survive these decision-filled days in the early life of the Australian Bookshop.

Chapter 9

CREATING THE BOOKSHOP

'A pile of rocks ceases to be a rock when somebody contemplates it
with the idea of a cathedral in mind.'

Antoine de Saint-Exupery

PARIS, 1996

It would have been very satisfying to see the ancient bookshop on the Quai des Grands Augustins restored to its former glory, but, after much deliberation, I decide that this could be intimidating for the average visitor who might lack the courage even to enter the shop, let alone open the glass doors of the shelves and take out the books. I love the beautiful old bookshops of Paris but I really need the Australian Bookshop to have an atmosphere that is more casual, more inviting and, if possible, totally different from any other bookshop in Paris.

David introduces me to some French friends of his who will do the painting, renovations and lighting. The first of these friends is Lionel, a sculptor and designer. I have already seen his beautiful woodwork below deck on the Chinese junk-boat *La Guinguette Pirate*, which is normally found floating on the Seine opposite the new Bibliothèque Nationale. Unlike some of the boats moored along the Seine, this *jonque* is seaworthy so from time to time it disappears. All kinds of events are held on the deck, especially during the long twilight evenings of summer and I have been there several times to listen to David and his friends making music.

108

Downstairs, the cabin of the junk is a warm, comfortable area with glowing wooden furnishings lovingly detailed by Lionel. Last summer he also created some large sculptures on the bank of the river beside *La Guinguette Pirate*. Crowds came along to hear the music and, because of a safety law, lest the boat should sink, some people had to be turned away. They didn't leave but sat along the banks and listened to the music. Afterwards some short films were shown in the shadow of Lionel's imposing sculptures. This scene remains clearly in my mind – a happy and unexpected occasion when music, art and leisure combined to create a joyful atmosphere; a lovely example of serendipity.

I am thrilled that the Australian Bookshop will also be situated beside the Seine, on the Left Bank among the bookshops, publishing houses and art galleries of the 6th arrondissement as well as the *bouquinistes* which line that part of the river. In summer the banks of the Seine come to life with all kinds of dancing and entertainment until the early hours of the morning. Twilight in summer can last until eleven o'clock and it's magical to stroll along the banks of the river in the evening cool. The light is a gentle blue and gold and the major buildings along the Seine are floodlit so that you have the impression of walking in the midst of a gigantic theatre set. There is an air of unreality that makes anything seem possible. At this time Paris has a quiet beauty, which is very seductive. It's a wonderful setting for the bookshop.

As I so admire Lionel's workmanship and appreciate his creativity, I decide to give him *carte blanche* for the furnishing of the bookshop – that is, he can freely use his imagination to design and supply the shelving, display cases and counter. I explain to him that, although the original bookshop must have been very beautiful, I want him to create a different atmosphere, where the books will almost appear to leap from the shelves so that people feel the urge to pick them up, look at them and, hopefully, buy them.

Two weeks later he shows me his designs, which are bold and certainly very different from anything I have ever seen. He suggests using wrought iron, oak and partly rusted corrugated iron. It's daring and I hesitate for a moment, wondering what on earth the purists might think. But when Lionel explains to me that he has been thinking of the red earth and green-grey bush of Australia and that the shelves will 'offer' the books to the customers, I decide to go ahead. His choice of corrugated iron is interesting, as he hasn't been to Australia and I don't think he has ever seen the work of Australian architect Glenn Murcutt, who also uses such pioneer materials in his designs.

❧ ☙

We decide, with the owner's permission, to remove the pale pink carpet and sand the floorboards. A pale pink carpet may have been pretty in a clothing boutique but it doesn't suit the image Lionel has of the Australian Bookshop. We do, however, decide to keep the Sarah Bernhardt wallpaper – it is so excessive that it gives an ordinary washroom and toilet an exotic, even slightly decadent look.

The work is to begin with the lifting of the carpet and on the morning the carpet is to be lifted in preparation for sanding the floorboards, I get up very early in order to meet Lionel at the bookshop with the key. Being a night person, I rarely see the sun rise, but on this occasion I am walking across the Pont des Arts when the sun bursts over the horizon amidst a cloud of iridescent rose- and golden-coloured light, which is reflected in the waters of the Seine. I think of Renoir's painting of the Pont des Arts and its gentle luminescence.

I am happy at the progress I have made and feel as though I'm floating on air. The Pont des Arts is, at any time of the day, a beautiful place to be. It's a *passerelle* (footbridge) and the original elegant iron bridge was built in 1803. It was damaged by barges and neglected for many years but in 1985 it was reconstructed using steel. Partly because the architecture is very light and pleasing to look at and partly because of its situation – looking back at the Île de la Cité and flanked by the Louvre on one side and the half-circle façade of the Palais de L'Institut on the other – the Pont des Arts has become a meeting place for artists, lovers and anyone else who appreciates its romantic atmosphere. On

July the fourteenth it is crowded because it's a good vantage point for viewing the annual fireworks display which emanates from the area around the Eiffel Tower.

While the sanding is in progress I stay away from the shop, fearing that the clouds of fine sawdust swirling through the air might cause an asthma attack, but David and Glenda, friends from Melbourne who have just arrived back in Paris, drop by my apartment to tell me that Lionel and his team seem to be having a good time, singing and joking as they work. Glenda is the bookseller from Melbourne who said she would help with the establishment of the bookshop while she is holidaying in France and she is true to her word. She and her husband, David, arrived in France last April and have been touring in the provinces. During my search for a shop she phoned me every week and now that the shop is on its way they are back in Paris, ready to lend a hand. I suggest that they keep on holidaying for a bit longer as we can't do anything at the shop until the floor is finished and the books are delivered.

෴ ෴

From now on there are not enough hours in the day as I juggle accommodation problems, shop renovations, visits of friends and family, dinner parties with people who want to be involved with the Australian Bookshop, meetings with Australian Embassy contacts, business details pertaining to transport and freight, customs, taxation, banks, lawyers, Telecom, the Post Office, endless visits to deposit business certificates here, there and everywhere – the list goes on and on. My middle child, Richard, told me in March that he was thinking of getting married in June. As he and Cait have lived together for some time this is not totally unexpected; of course I want to be there but the timing isn't the best! When the invitation arrives I hesitate, partly because of the expense but mainly because so much is happening in Paris, but in the end, I leave Lionel and his team to their work and rush back to Australia for a few days. It turns out that Richard and Cait have decided to honeymoon in Paris and, quite by chance, we all return on the same plane and we have some happy times together in Paris.

When I get back the floor is finished and it looks wonderful, so I congratulate the workers and Lionel goes back to his home in the country to finish making the furnishings he has designed. In the meantime the walls are painted white and Daniel Levy comes in to design the lighting. Daniel is a talented young Frenchman with a friendly manner and a charming smile. He designs lighting for theatrical and musical productions and is well known for his innovative ideas.

Daniel looks at Lionel's designs and asks me a few questions regarding the aims of the Australian Bookshop. I quote from the *Statuts*, twenty-eight *articles* (regulations) for the creation of a company, which have been signed and deposited at 6 rue Saint-Hyacinthe, as required. The Australian Bookshop is registered as a company with the following aim:

Achat, vente de livres, disques, cassettes, neufs ou d'occasions, et de tout autre support ou prestation de service visant à promouvoir la culture australienne en particulier et toute autre culture en général.

Roughly translated this means:

The buying, selling of books, CDs, cassettes, new or second-hand, and supplying any other support services concerning the promotion of Australian culture in particular and all other culture in general.

My contact at the French Chamber of Commerce helped me with the wording and it seems to cover everything.

After some thought, Daniel suggests that we treat the books as the stars of the show, with little theatre lights around the tops of the shelves and hidden spotlights inside the original shelving to illuminate the books on the new shelves in front. For the overhead lighting he suggests two fluorescent lights – clear for the daylight hours and a pale rose for evenings – to enhance the colours on the covers of the books. In the empty back room he puts moveable spotlights for the photographs and paintings we hope to display there. Lionel installs the furnishings and it's all beginning to look a bit eccentric, but I like the effect and also like the idea of giving young French artists freedom to imagine and interpret as they wish.

The last of Lionel's work is the sign, which will hang above the front door. It's a work of art – a rusty sheet of corrugated iron, slightly larger than the width of the doorway, with the words 'Australian Bookshop' roughly cut out with a blowtorch. It's simple, unique and should work well because it can be seen from the far bank of the Seine and looks interesting enough to give people the urge to come inside, or so I hope. Lionel's furnishings are stunning and I can't wait to put the books on the shelves.

cs@ @s

The two French businesswomen have guided me through negotiations with the owner of the shop and some of the masses of French administration and paperwork I have had to deal with; David and his friends have held my hand whenever I needed it; Jacques has been there the whole time, offering kindness and practical help but, in the end, it is Glenda's energy, enthusiasm and experience which give me sufficient strength to bring the shop to life.

She comes every day to the shop and throws herself wholeheartedly into the business of buying equipment and planning the opening. We fill the whole of the display windows with large signs, one window in French and the other in English, saying: Australian Bookshop – Opening Soon – Visit Australia Here and *À Bientôt Pour L'Ouverture, L'Australie, C'est Ici.* The latter may not be good French but is good free publicity, because buses and cars pass here daily, not to mention the hordes of tourists walking to and from Notre Dame and the Gare D'Orsay and the French families meandering past the *bouquinistes* on Sunday afternoons.

One day Glenda and I take the train out to the suburbs, past the *périphérique*, to where there is a huge warehouse selling office supplies. I have already bought a computer so our main purpose today is to buy a cheap cash register. The whole reason for shopping out here in the suburbs is to save money, which can then be spent on extra books, but at the end of the afternoon we look at each other and burst out laughing. We have ended up buying a stepladder and various other bits and pieces as well. We can't possibly carry these large articles so to return by train is out of the question. We decide that we must order a large taxi; this is easier said than done and takes a long, long time, partly because I haven't yet learned that here in France a large taxi is called a *break* and partly because there aren't many taxis available so far out from central Paris.

The bookshop phone is now connected and we both concentrate hard on our French, especially when phone numbers are delivered at full-speed, like the rat-a-tat-tat of a machine gun. On one occasion I return to the shop and Glenda tells me that she has just taken down another 'mad message'.

'What is it?' I ask.

'Your rocks will be delivered by barge tomorrow.'

'Which rocks? I haven't ordered any rocks!'

We both have an image of a huge pile of rocks floating down the Seine towards the Australian Bookshop until I remember the storage shelves for the private back room. To save money, I decided to use bricks and planks of wood and I forgot that my helpful friend Jacques said he would find some bricks for me. He has done so and has asked

his friend, Françoise, to phone and tell me that it is all
arranged. They are indeed coming by barge, but the landing
is further down the river and he will collect them and
deliver them here by car.

Jacques has been a wonderful friend and is always ready
with ideas and practical aid. He finds me a filing cabinet,
lends me some furniture for the back room and is always
there to listen if there is a problem. He came to Paris in
1968 to work at UNESCO, so his experience and advice
are invaluable. With his and Maria's continuing emotional
support, as well as that of my family, I am richly endowed.

⤳ ⤶

The first load of books from Australia will be delivered in a
week's time, on 11 July, so I am beginning to think about
ordering translations from French publishers when suddenly
the gods smile upon me, yet again. A young French woman
comes into the shop, tells me how much she loves Australian
literature, cinema, in fact everything about Australia and
offers to help on Saturdays and Sundays. This is Claire de
Robespierre. I couldn't have wished for more dedicated or
talented fellow workers than Claire and Glenda and they
are the first of a long list of people who offer their services
voluntarily because they too feel passionate about the idea
of an Australian bookshop in Paris. The project seems to be
gathering momentum as opening day comes closer.

Claire tells me that she studied Australian cinema, concentrating on '*Gallipoli* and the Image of the Anzacs' for her doctorate, which she has just completed at the Sorbonne under the supervision of Professor Jean-Claude Redonnet. She says that when she began studying Australia she entered a world she hadn't known existed. Although many died on the battlefields of France, she hadn't known that Australians fought in World War I and it was only through the study of the film *Gallipoli* that she discovered the history, traditions and culture of Australia. Reading books about Australian cinema led her to other Australian books and to a great love of Australia, especially its open spaces and its nature.

Claire has an important job with one of Paris' top literary agents, Michelle Lapautre, so she has an excellent knowledge of books in general, but her knowledge of Australian literature and cinema is astounding. She tells me that she tries to spend a month every year travelling in Australia. She has already seen much more of Australia than most Australians and takes beautiful photographs wherever she goes. It will be great to have her at the Australian Bookshop on Saturdays and Sundays, when I'm sure there will be lots of people asking about tourism as well as books because there is no Australian Tourist Office in France.

During the past ten years I have compiled a basic list of Australian books translated into French and now I sub-scribe to *Livres Hebdo*, a weekly trade magazine that lists all books published in France and Claire and I comb publishers' catalogues for Australian translations. I know I have met a kindred spirit because she seems to enjoy reading the catalogues as much as I do and loves talking about books – Australian books in particular.

Beneath her quiet exterior, Claire has strength of character and great integrity – she is honest and reliable and very determined. I'm sure she will be very successful in her career at the literary agency and am enormously grateful that she wants to devote her spare time to the Australian Bookshop. She takes over the ordering of the French books and supervises my local letter writing, which is a huge relief as I am not at all confident in my ability to write polite business letters in French. Her opinions and guidance are invaluable, not only because of her personal experience but also because she is an active member of a Franco–Australian group, Antipodes, which promotes Australian cinema.

I have noticed that many French publishers do not work through literary agents and that most of the literary agents in France deal only with translations of foreign books into French. This observation is affirmed by several articles I read in *Livres Hebdo*. With a few exceptions, the agents in Paris represent foreign agencies, publishers and writers and sell books which have already appeared in other languages. They are often sub-agents for large overseas agencies or publishing houses. A few of them represent authors but at present these are exceptions. The French publishers appear to prefer developing a relationship directly with the foreign authors and most French authors don't have agents. This is gradually changing as French writers become aware of the possibilities of negotiating sales of film and electronic rights.

Agent Laura Fountain tells me that when she created her agency in Paris in 1985 she was unable to write *agent littéraire* as her job description because there was no such category in the lists of jobs registered with the Taxation Office. Boris Hoffman's agency, Agence Hoffman, was established in 1935 so I suppose they must have described themselves as literary consultants.

cൟ ർ

Now that the books are arriving we must begin pricing them so I go again to the Centre national du livre (National Centre for the Book) to collect information on the pricing of imported books. Because in France literature is regarded as a social necessity, the Centre national du livre is a state-funded institution that supports writers, translators, publishers, bookshops, libraries and literary associations. It also supports, along with other public and private sponsors, the Maison des écrivains (the Writers' House) which describes itself as a 'meeting place for French and foreign writers, a space for reflection upon the role of the writer today'. I love this description and the house itself, which is a wonderful old *hôtel particulier* (private mansion) situated at 55 rue de Verneuil in the 7th arrondissement. Rue de Verneuil is a quiet, paved street with many cultural connections and some interesting architecture, some of which has survived from the eighteenth century.

You enter the Maison des écrivains through an impressive arched gateway; on the left is a small building occupied by the Café des Lettres – a charming restaurant hosted by a warm and friendly Swedish woman. On sunny days it's very pleasant eating at tables in the courtyard, which leads to the front steps of the house itself, a fairytale jewel that invites you to enter. Seen from the courtyard, the rooms seem large and elegant, in proportion to the graceful old building. There are many of these beautiful old mansions devoted to various aspects of culture and they reflect the desire of the French Government to support the arts. It's a long and enviable tradition.

I study again the law concerning the pricing of both French and Australian books. I say 'again' because I already obtained this information when I was in Australia. As I thought, it is easy for the French books because the prices are fixed, thanks to the law of 10 August 1981 (I've heard

37. Vieux Paris. — La place Saint-André-des-Arts.

this referred to as 'Jack Lang's law' as he was the colourful Minister for Culture at the time the law was passed). This law (*prix unique*) means that a book must be sold at the same price by all bookshops. A discount of up to 5 per cent *may* be charged but even even the big department stores and major chains like FNAC cannot reduce the price of a new book by any more than 5 per cent. This law was adopted to protect small independent booksellers.

I see that, by law, the importer of a book from another country must charge the same price as the price decided on by the first person to import the book so I phone the Centre du livre for clarification of this law and am told that I should 'just ask the publishers'.

'But these books are Australian and the publishers will have no idea what price they'll be in Europe,' I argue.

'Well then, you'll have to find out who first imported each book and use the same price as they have.'

I am astonished and eventually decide that there is absolutely no way of doing this and that not many Australian books seem to have reached France, anyway. I will just have to factor in costs of handling, transport, customs and taxes to arrive at a reasonable price. This is difficult – if the books are too expensive no one will buy them and if we don't charge enough we won't make any profit. As it is, a well-known French anthropologist comes in one day while we are getting ready, takes a look at the books already on the shelves and informs me that my prices are too high. He has often travelled to Australia so knows the Australian prices, but hasn't stopped to think of the costs involved in flying the books to France.

The TVA, the French equivalent of England's VAT (Value added tax), is another problem – it is only 5.5 per cent for books but other paper goods, such as cards, maps, bookmarks and mobiles, seem to attract a variety of different taxes, up to 20.6 per cent. (Friends have suggested stocking a few of these items for the backpackers who might not want to carry heavy books.) After spending a whole day researching the many different TVA codes, I decide to follow a French colleague's advice: 'Put all your sales dockets in a shoebox and hand them over to an expert accountant. Let him work out the TVA. You'll have more than enough to do.'

Other French friends have also recommended an accountant, so I decide to do as the French do and employ an *expert-comptable* to set up the financial side of things. I'm not happy with the first one and soon change to another bigger company, recommended by the French Chamber of Commerce. They offer to send someone to the shop each month to pick up the necessary documents and cheques for payment of the many obligatory taxes on French businesses. This makes life easier, although my helpers are all horrified at the large amount I will have to pay each month to French Government departments. The health and retirement benefits are excellent in France but the public pays heavily for them, especially small businesses. About this time I hear of a number of French companies establishing themselves in the UK and Belgium simply to avoid start-up costs. Of course, the Government here frowns upon this and says they will do their best to stop it.

∽◉ ◉〜

It's been a great team effort and with the help of Claire and Glenda I am able to quietly open the Australian Bookshop in early August, before the official opening ceremonies. This gives us the opportunity to slowly create and adapt a solid routine that should prove useful in the days ahead, which already seem as though they might be busier than I first anticipated when I dreamed up the idea of an Australian bookshop in Paris so many years ago.

Chapter 10

LE LANCEMENT (OPENING WEEK)

'I was wandering Paris alone and one day came across the Australian Bookshop. From memory, it was still being fitted out. Perhaps it wasn't even open for business yet. But I walked in, curious, and met Elaine. She was . . . improbable. I mean, the situation was improbable. A shop dealing only with Australian literature, on the Left Bank – how on earth would it survive?'

Luke Davies

PARIS, SEPTEMBER 1996

I am in my sixtieth year and very excited because tonight is the first of four receptions planned to celebrate the opening of my long-dreamed-of Australian Bookshop in Paris. Initially I had planned only one opening event but the list of guests was so long I decided to have two opening parties. Then the Australian Embassy phoned to say that writers Gillian Bouras and Herb Wharton were both in town and would like to read this week. One of the main objectives of the Australian Bookshop is to support visiting Australian authors so I agreed, and here we are, beginning what has become a week of opening celebrations.

Tonight the official opening will be performed by the Australian Ambassador, Alan Brown, and on Tuesday evening Austrade's good-humoured and hard-working Sallyanne Atkinson will be the guest of honour at another 'inaugural evening'. This will be followed by a *rencontre* (encounter) with Gillian Bouras on Wednesday and another *rencontre* with Herb Wharton on Friday. It's a big programme and only possible because of the Australian Bookshop's team of helpers.

Australian publishers have co-operated, export, visa and customs problems have been painstakingly negotiated and French friends have pulled out all stops to have the shop ready for this week – it looks fantastic.

Lionel's imaginative renovations are complete and an eclectic selection of Australian books is almost dancing off the bookshelves, their colourful dust jackets dazzlingly lit by Daniel's theatrical lighting. Having a choice of two kinds of overhead lighting ensures the books always look their best – bright, natural lighting for everyday use and, for the evenings, soft, rose-coloured lighting which, as Daniel predicted, brilliantly enhances the colours on the covers of the books. Daniel normally works with actors and musicians but tonight the stars of this show are the books.

It's a far cry from the rows of white or cream-covered books with neat, black lettering commonly found in French bookshops. And deliberately so: Paris is a very big city with thousands of bookshops so a new, small bookshop like the Australian Bookshop needs to be very distinctive to make any impression. I was intrigued to find that the titles and authors' names on the spines of French published books run from bottom to top, whereas ours go in the opposite direction, so that you turn your head to the left to read the French spines and to the right when reading the titles of books written in English. As I have placed the translations beside the original editions of the books, I imagine heads will be bobbing in all directions this evening.

Lionel has created some beautiful curved *fer forgé*

(wrought iron) supports to hold the waxed oak shelves which are in descending tiers in front of the old shelves. The words 'wrought iron' do not do justice to Lionel's work. Under the rose-tinted lighting, the *fer forgé* is a soft, metallic grey in colour but it has been beaten so that smooth, tiny little ridges all over it give a rippled effect which makes you want to touch it. The moveable display counter in the middle of the shop is also of waxed oak and its doors of beaten and aged copper evoke the red earth of Central Australia and the misty, blue-green eucalypt forests found in many other parts of Australia.

Lionel is justifiably proud of his work, so I asked him whether he would like to write a short description of it. He becomes quite poetic and this is what is displayed on the back wall of the bookshop:

> 'Surgissant de l'ancienne bibliothèque,
> des pieds d'acier s'avancent vers nous.
> Ils nous offrent sur des plateaux de
> chêne ciré une vision de l'univers
> australien.
> Les matériaux donnent un spectacle
> brut et authentique.
> La mise en scène est réalisée par le
> sculpteur-décorateur Lionel CLAUDE.
> La pâtine du temps crée la matière qui

joue avec le regard pour nous livrer
une émotion atemporelle.'

This can be translated as:

'Surging from the ancient bookshop,
feet of steel come towards us.
They offer us, on shelves of
waxed oak, a vision of the Australian
universe.
The materials used give a look
that is rough and authentic.
This setting was created by the
sculptor-decorator Lionel CLAUDE.
The patina of time evoked by these materials
plays with our vision to give us
a timeless feeling.'

It seems that Lionel, along with many other French people I've met, sees Australia as exotic and other-wordly. 'Other-worldly' could also describe the way I'm feeling this evening at the first of our opening ceremonies. Only last year I was in Australia, preparing the dossier and negotiating terms with publishers and now here I am in my Australian Bookshop on the Left Bank with its shelves of books in French and English, its stunning furnishings and lighting,

the crowds of people spilling out onto the footpath attracting much attention from passers-by. The Quai des Grands
Augustins looks romantic in the evening light, with Notre
Dame cathedral and the spire of the Sainte Chapelle visible
from the front door and the searchlights of the *bateaux-
mouches* sweeping over us at regular intervals, creating a
scrim-like backdrop as they trace the delicate outlines of the
branches of the plane trees that line the Seine.

Tonight we even have a photographic exhibition. A
French photographer, Michel Fainsilber, came by last week
with his collection of Australian photographs. They are now
on display in the back room and the stunning black and
white portraits add to the atmosphere because the faces are
uniquely Australian. Michel travelled in outback Australia –
mainly in the Northern Territory and Broome – and has
captured a series of rugged, individual portraits of people
who can only be described as eccentric outback characters.
Their lived-in faces are powerful symbols of the harshness
of some outback lives and the French guests, particularly,
are fascinated by them. Some Australians here have already
recognised friends or acquaintances and are intrigued to see
them hanging on the walls of a bookshop on the Left Bank
in Paris.

The children's books, displayed in the original glass-
fronted bookshelf just inside the door, have also attracted
attention. Thanks to Glenda's expert advice, we have an

outstanding collection of Australian children's books and I am proud of the beautifully illustrated covers, which can be seen from the street. Glenda and I made a conscious decision to place the children's corner at the front of the shop and it is certainly attracting much more attention than if it were placed at the back. Soon, however, there are so many guests that it's becoming difficult to see the books at all.

The shop is already full and the Ambassador has not yet arrived. I'm thankful that the back room is open to the public. Lionel's friends have supplied beautifully decorated *canapés* and *petit fours* as well as *pain surprise*. The magnums of champagne donated by Moët et Chandon are rapidly disappearing. Moët et Chandon were generous and asked how much champagne I needed but I have greatly under-estimated the attendance numbers and their capacity to drink champagne on a hot night.

Moët et Chandon have a vineyard in Australia, just outside Melbourne, but the other important Australian connection tonight is the Moët et Chandon Australian Art Foundation, inaugurated in 1987. Maudie Palmer is presently the Foundation Director and the Fellow this year is urban Aboriginal artist Judy Watson, who is here with her parents for the opening of the bookshop. She has won the prize of AU$50,000 cash and a year's residency at a studio located in the historic surroundings of the Abbey of Hautvillers, a part of the House of Moët et Chandon, at

Epernay in Champagne. In appreciation of their generosity at all levels, we have a display counter explaining the Foundation and showcasing their beautiful catalogues of Judy Watson's paintings. Tonight we celebrate her success.

We are also celebrating the success of Australian author Bernard Cohen, who is on the shortlist for *The Australian/ Vogel* prize with the manuscript of his first novel, *The Blindman's Hat*, so on the other side of the display counter is an explanation of the Vogel alongside some examples of other books by previous Vogel winners, including *An Open Swimmer* by Tim Winton, *Lillian's Story* by Kate Grenville, *The Mint Lawn* by Gillian Mears and *Praise* by Andrew McGahan. The Vogel is Australia's richest prize for an unpublished manuscript – it's promoted by *The Australian* newspaper and Allen & Unwin organise the administration of the award and guarantee to publish the manuscript.

Bernard and his wife, Nicola, are staying in the Keesing Studio, at the Cité Internationale des Arts and they have been in and out of the bookshop all week, sometimes to send faxes and sometimes just to chat. For Glenda, Claire and me, it's been interesting and exciting to share part of their Paris experience. Bernard says he's been writing for many years and this is his first real recognition, so this stay in Paris is a milestone in his writing career.

The Cité Internationale des Arts is a fascinating concept

and a great example of how much value is placed on the arts by the French. It was founded in 1965 when the City of Paris donated the land and the French Government gave financial support. But the idea was proposed in 1947 by Felix Brunau, a French diplomat who noticed that after World War II the high rents in the city were deterring artists. He and his wife lobbied for the establishment of a non-profit-making international arts centre and Madame Simone Brunau still manages the place and interviews every artist who comes there. She is a forceful personality and some artists await the interview with fear and trembling, uncertain of their reception. Madame Brunau is elderly now but her spirit is strong, as is her belief in the value of bringing artists in many fields and from many countries to gather together in Paris, to work, to discuss and exchange ideas, to contribute to each other's development and to absorb all that Paris has to offer as one of the world's great centres of artistic expression.

There are more than 300 studios within the complex, leased by government and non-government organisations from forty-five countries. At least six of the studios are leased by Australian organisations; the Australian writers' studio, administered by the Australia Council, is known as the Nancy Keesing Studio in honour of the Australian writer who bequeathed funding for the studio in memory of her parents.

Another guest of honour at this first party is the owner of the shop, M. Vinarnic, who arrives with his wife and presents me with a ceramic model of the Australian Bookshop. He says that he and the tenants above the shop are very happy that the old nineteenth-century building once again contains a bookshop. He came by earlier today and, standing at the door, scattered a handful of coins around the shop, 'for good luck,' he told me. Later this afternoon a large potted palm tree was delivered, another gift from M. Vinarnic. Each branch was decorated with little bags of 'gold' coins (actually bronze *centimes*) and the whole thing was topped off with French and Australian flags.

It's a convivial Franco–Australian evening. The Australian Ambassador, Alan Brown, makes a speech welcoming our French guests in particular. M. Jean-Paul Delamotte says that he too is delighted that the Australian Bookshop is here to add to the efforts he and his wife, Monique, have made over the past twenty years to promote Australian literature in France. Representatives of the other Franco–Australian groups murmur their good wishes, French friends and colleagues offer words of encouragement, expats greet each other and the first party's away.

It is becoming quite hot in the shop, even though it's autumn, but there are at least seventy people here. The two rooms can only comfortably hold fifty people, so we place some chairs outside on the footpath, facing the Seine. My friend Maria sits outside when the heat becomes too much for her and others soon join her. Glenda, David, Claire, Jacques and Françoise all help distribute food and drink and chat with people. As well as assisting with the delivery of our 'rocks', Françoise organised the paper bags and office stationery for us. She also rang at the last minute, very anxiously, to enquire whether I had a suitable outfit to wear for the opening. Very French! Glenda answered the phone and told her that she shouldn't worry because I had recently attended two weddings.

People don't seem to want to leave and the French guests ask lots of questions so I suppose that's the sign of a merry and successful party. Steve McLeod of SBS Television has the last word – in our *livre d'or* (visitors' book) he writes: 'I've always wanted to write something in France – this is it.' As for me, I'm very happy and hope that the interest shown tonight augers well for the future.

⁂

The second opening party, on the following Tuesday, is just as busy as the first and again we run out of champagne. A quick call to Australian importer Vinnie Laing sees the Moët et Chandon magnums replaced with an Australian version of champagne made by the same company in the Yarra Valley near Melbourne. It's called Green Point Vintage Brut (1993) and the French guests express surprise that such good 'champagne' can be made in Australia (even though we are now obliged to call it 'sparkling wine'). It is 1996 and they are only just beginning to find out that Australian wines can compete successfully in the world market place. Sallyanne Atkinson does the honours tonight and she is wonderfully encouraging and supportive. There are about fifty people here and it is a little more comfortable than last Thursday. The atmosphere is relaxed, some members of the press attend, the team of helpers is back again and the Australian Bookshop is well and truly christened.

On Wednesday evening, Australian author Gillian Bouras is the guest reader and she begins what we hope will become a pattern of events at the bookshop. As the Australian Bookshop cannot afford to bring writers over from Australia, the plan is to present writers who are either visiting Paris or are temporarily residing in the Nancy Keesing Studio at the Cité Internationale des Arts.

The word *rencontre* means 'meeting' (in the sense of 'getting together') or 'encounter' and I'm hoping these will be exchanges of ideas rather than formal readings. I propose calling them the '*Au bout du monde*' series of *rencontres*. Paris has a great history of *rencontres*, many of which take the form of *cafés littéraires*. The idea of the Australian Bookshop has evolved over the years and I have come to believe more than ever in the importance of giving Australian writers a voice in Paris. In Sydney I used to go to readings at the Harold Park Hotel and found that although they were not always comfortable, they gave me some insights into the specific problems faced by Indigenous Australian writers. People here know so little about Australia – perhaps the *rencontres* will give them some insights into the Australian way of being.

Gillian Bouras is the perfect person to begin the tradition because, although born in Melbourne, she lived in Greece for many years and this evening she tells us that she has now become a nomad, bridging the two cultures. She introduces her books: *A Foreign Wife*, *Aphrodite and the Others* and *A Fair Exchange*. Her descriptions of the difficulties and pleasures of adjusting to a new country with a young family are moving and for me Gillian becomes another of those women who inspire others to take the plunge and experience new ways of living.

On the following Friday, Herb Wharton is the guest of honour. Herb is a raconteur and he sits in my Norwegian leather captain's chair (a good-luck symbol I gave myself shortly after I was divorced) in the far corner of the shop and yarns about his days as a stockman, droving from the north of Australia down to Adelaide in the south and working on cattle stations. His books – *Unbranded*, *Cattle Camp* and *Where Ya Been Mate?* – are full of outback stories and those he recounts tonight are enthusiastically received by people who know little about the size of Australia and even less about its Indigenous population. Still, it's a start, and I am happy that so many Parisians have responded to the invitations. At least they know where to find us and at best they will come back to look at the rest of the books and maybe even buy them.

Chapter 11

EARLY DAYS – 'OU EST LE KOALA?'

'To step into the Australian Bookshop was to feel instantly at home in Paris and at the same time, to see Australia in a new light. It was such an ambitious and daring venture, and Elaine was always so warm, enthusiastic and encouraging.'

Fiona Capp

PARIS, 1996

The Australian Bookshop is still in its infancy but I've already made friends with some of the neighbours who live on the Quai des Grands Augustins – they have made me very welcome and I am beginning to feel a sense of belonging and that all my dreams have come true. Often I see Madame Joyeux, who lives in the apartment above, leaving the building, still looking like the star she once was; she will often emerge upon the arm of an elderly escort, dressed expensively, her hair beautifully coloured and coiffed, just as though she is about to walk onto the stage of the Comédie Française. If, by chance, it is raining, she will politely ask whether she can wait in the Bookshop until the taxi comes. She is, indeed, a *grande dame*. I have a small souvenir of her which I found in Melbourne – a second-hand copy of her book, *Child of the Ballet* (*Côté Jardin*), translated by Arnold Haskell and published in 1952. In it she describes her days at the school of the Paris Opéra Ballet when she was one of *les petits rats*, as they affectionately called the young students. She came to the official opening, as did several other neighbours. Andrew, a charming and debonair Englishman who lives further down the quai, comes in often to browse and discuss Australia, where he lived for about six years, and Elizabeth, a Frenchwoman who lives in the 16th and is a lover of all things English, comes in regularly to buy books and to talk.

Hanna, who walks by the shop each day with her beautiful Alsatian, Dido, has begun coming in for a chat. Although she is presently living in Paris, Hanna's real home is in Tel Aviv and I don't think she has any special interest in Australian writers. English is her second language and she speaks it perfectly, so we converse in English.

One day I ask her why she came into the shop for the first time. She says, 'It looked such a warm, cosy and inviting place that I wanted to come in and see what was happening. This first impression has lingered in my mind – I feel welcome and at ease, especially in such a strange city.'

I don't know whether to be sad or happy when another regular visitor, Alain, tells me that he has just spoken with one of his friends in Brisbane, who said, 'There are only two people in the world I envy – my husband's mistress and that woman who has just opened the Australian Bookshop in Paris.'

So many people tell me that they have always wanted to open a bookshop in Paris that I begin to feel as though I'm living out other people's dreams as well as my own. I thought I might feel deflated after the excitement of the opening festivities, but there isn't time to think about anything because we have been inundated with customers, journalists and tourists – and the letters!

Following publicity in *The Bulletin*, *The Australian*, *The Age* and *The Australian Way* (Qantas inflight magazine), as well as some Australian writers' magazines, I have received an avalanche of letters from all kinds of interesting people. Some want me to sell their books, some have even sent manuscripts or translations and others have simply written to say 'Congratulations!'. It's exciting but I don't know when I'm going to be able to answer them all because there is a mountain of things to be done each day. We are ordering new books from Australia and responding to people wanting us to advertise through them; negotiating with tourist offices wanting to liaise with us; not to mention dealing with the new accountant, the bank, deliveries from Australia, the UK and France, visits from book reps and on and on it goes.

I'm so glad Glenda is here during the week to support me and steer me through this teething stage. Glenda, too, is pleasantly surprised by the response and says, 'You know, I have a feeling that it's always going to be busy like this.'

❧ ❧

One day a young woman comes into the bookshop and tells me and Glenda that she represents a certain third world government, which has allocated a large amount of money to buy books in English. She says that they are particularly interested in Australian books and goes around the shop pulling out the books she says she intends to buy. To begin with, we are excited about this huge sale but, as time passes, I become suspicious. I say that the books cannot leave the shop until they are paid for. She gives me what seem genuine French Government phone numbers and I speak to various people who assure me, in French, that what she says is true – it is part of an aid package. She ends up with about five cartons of books but I remain adamant that they cannot leave the shop until I receive a cash payment. She departs and, of course, never returns. Some of the other Australians with businesses in Paris tell me that they, too, have been subjected to similar scams when they first set up their businesses.

During this first month we have been visited by a lot of Australian tourists and they all seem thrilled to find an Australian bookshop on the Left Bank and become instant experts advising us about their favourite books. The problem is, although we enjoy talking to them, the time passes all too quickly and they don't buy any books. This I understand, because books are very heavy to carry, especially if you're trying to travel light as many of our visitors are. We can only hope they spread the word in other countries and places. There are a lot of French visitors as well and I'm thankful that Claire is here on Saturdays and Sundays – it's wonderful to be able to leave most of the talking to her for those two days, as I find speaking in French all day every day very tiring and can only hope I'll feel more relaxed as time goes by.

One of the reasons we are much busier than I had anticipated is because the shop is on the tourist track between Notre Dame and the Gare d'Orsay. The impressive amount of publicity generated by the opening festivities helps too. We are beginning to make connections all around the world and I think of them as threads, linking all kinds of people to the Australian Bookshop, in our own small worldwide web.

We've had numerous requests for books that are not in stock so, following Glenda's suggestion, we list all of the books with the names and addresses and telephone numbers of those who request them. As we order the new books our list of suppliers expands very quickly, adding to the paperwork. We also begin another list of Parisian customers who have expressed interest in coming to *rencontres*, which may be readings, art and music events or whatever seems a good idea at the time. Fortunately we have a programme on the computer that enables us to make these lists and the list of books in stock more easily than if we had to do it all by hand. As soon as a book is sold, the number in stock is adjusted – we can't afford to be fully automated but our system seems to be working well, even though we are kept busy when the books come in.

We soon have a long list of customers and, although I'm feeling thrilled at the interest aroused, I can't help but wonder how I will manage when Glenda goes. (Both Glenda and Claire are working voluntarily because of their shared passion for books, and we are always busy.) It's exciting but a bit nerve-racking. We don't have a moment's rest during the day so, when I should be sleeping, I find myself thinking about all the things that need to be done the next day. It's impossible to do the paperwork during opening hours, so I sit in the shop at night and work until 9 or 10 pm and then have a meal on the way home, usually *moules et frites, steak et frites* or a *grill mixte*, washed down with a glass of red wine.

It's a period of adjustment for me – from twenty-five years of academia to the business world; from what is thought of here as the New World in the antipodes to the Old World in Europe; and from my mother tongue to the French language, which I have always loved, but have never used for any length of time. As well, it's back to working very long hours, something I haven't done for the past five or six years.

✧ ✧

One of the reasons for the constant flow of customers may be an article about the first opening party which appeared in *Le Figaro*, one of Paris' daily broadsheet newspaper, with a readership of 350,000. Fortunately or unfortunately, depending upon one's point of view, the article began with a description of a stuffed koala that was propping open the front door of the bookshop when journalist Caroline Fouché came by. Now whenever I try to hide the wretched animal in the back room someone comes in and says, '*Mais où est le koala?*' (Where's the koala?) *Le Figaro* seems to have a large number of readers in the provinces because already several country people have come to visit us, producing the newspaper clipping they have saved for their next visit to Paris and they, too, ask after the koala. The said animal was donated to the Australian Bookshop by a young French friend during the opening week preparations and we didn't quite know what to do with it so it was placed by the door with a pair of spectacles perched on its strangely pointed nose. It seems destined to remain there.

A photographer from the newspaper had taken some photos at the opening party and Mlle Fouché wanted more details in order to write an article which appeared a few days later. Headed by a photograph of Ambassador Alan Brown standing in front of one of Lionel's bookshelves, the article speaks of the 'richness of Australian literature, with its mixture of writing by immigrants from many parts of the world as well as by the original inhabitants of the country'.

She also described Lionel's efforts at creating an 'Australian' atmosphere by his use of rusty corrugated iron and praised the artistry of his wrought iron. He should be very pleased and, happily for us, it also mentions the *rencontres* with Gillian Bouras and Herb Wharton the following week, which may explain the good attendance at these two events.

This is the kind of publicity we need if we are to attract French customers, which is my main aim. Australian expats probably won't buy many books as they will have contacts in Australia who can supply them with whatever they need, without attracting customs duty and taxes, so our target must be the French, and, idealistically speaking, one of the major reasons for having an Australian bookshop in Paris is to give Australian writers a voice in the international community.

There has been a lot of other free publicity for the Australian Bookshop – I certainly haven't needed to spend AU$30,000 on advertising, as suggested by Austrade, because there are already more customers than I can manage on my own. Glenda will soon be returning to Australia and I can't possibly afford to engage anyone because, as well as the wage, there would be at least 40 per cent extra needed for taxes. When preparing the business plan I envisaged a small, one-person bookshop so I didn't factor in money for hiring help.

I can't spend time training a work-experience student (*un stagiaire*) because the work here is too specialised. Our customers expect us to know a lot about Australian books, cinema and art and, with the exception of Claire de Robespierre, few French students or post-graduates have that kind of knowledge. The Olympic Games, to be held in Sydney in 2000, have added to the rush of general interest in Australian culture. I hadn't thought of this when I did the market research in 1994 but it adds significantly to the more specialised interest displayed by universities and a number of private individuals. This is certainly the right time to take advantage of both past and future interest.

～⑤ ⑥～

Because of the successful *rencontres* with Gillian Bouras and Herb Wharton, I'm looking forward to organising many more such literary salons. Jean-Paul Delamotte introduces me to a young friend of his, William La Ganza, and suggests that I might like to organise a poetry reading for him. Although Jean-Paul has published him, I have not yet read Bill's poems, so decide to meet him to suggest that we organise an introduction to Australian poetry, which may include some of his work. We design an invitation for a *rencontre* called 'Introducing Australian Poets' and choose a selection of well-known poets 'from Banjo Paterson to contemporary poets such as Kevin Hart, David Malouf, John Tranter, Gwen Harwood, Les Murray . . .'. It's difficult to choose and the time will be limited, so we try to present those Australian poets whose work is already available in our 'Poets' Corner'.

By amazing coincidence, Australian poet Kevin Hart arrives in Paris a week before the poetry evening. His is to be a brief visit and he can't stay for the scheduled poetry *rencontre* at which his poetry will be featured. Harriet O'Malley of the Australian Embassy suggests we host '*un pot autour de* Kevin Hart' – literally, 'a drink around Kevin Hart'. I do a quick ring-around of friends and some of the customers, and the following evening, on 10 October, here we are, in the bookshop, celebrating the works of one of Australia's favourite poets. Bernard Cohen is present and Kevin Hart graciously invites him to read as well. It is an impromptu occasion and the atmosphere is relaxed and friendly, so good conversation follows the readings and we repair to what is becoming our favourite little restaurant in rue Hautefeuille to eat, drink and talk some more.

William La Ganza's poetry evening is well attended and very well received. He sits in the poetry corner, on the Norwegian leather captain's chair and reads a varied collection of Australian poetry including a couple of his own poems. I am delighted that poet June Shenfield (former owner of Cannibal Pierce, the first Australian bookshop in Paris) has come because I have been trying to contact her for some time. After the reading, a few of us are sitting around talking when she begins to weep and says, 'Oh, why couldn't they have done all this for us?' I try to explain that 'they' have not done anything for me either and that I have established the shop and paid for the drinks this evening with my own savings. I suggest that perhaps we can work

151

together but she is too distressed to listen. She is so sad that my heart goes out to her but there seems nothing I can do.

This evening is also a kind of farewell for David and Glenda, whose cheerfulness and practical help has carried me through these first two months. I will miss them so much but, as someone said to me, 'It's like that in Paris – just as you become close to someone they move away. It's always *bonjour* and *au revoir*.'

Glenda's voluntary dedication to the Australian Bookshop has been such that Jean-Paul thinks she is my sister. Not everyone understands people who give so generously and expect no return save the pleasure of giving – I feel devastated at saying goodbye to both David and Glenda and words can never fully express my gratitude to them. It's going to be hard work now that they have gone but I hope it will be manageable because of their input during the early days. And I still have Claire's enthusiasm at weekends.

⊂ᑎᕣ Ꮫᑎ⊃

I am alone in the shop during the week now and the days are very long. Nevertheless, the variety of people who visit the shop keeps me buoyant and optimistic. Most of the customers want me to talk about the books and help them choose. It's fortunate that I'm a quick reader so have read most of the books in stock, and I learn a lot from Claire as she, too, is an avid reader and likes to talk about what she has read. If we are excited about a book it is easy to make a sale because our excitement rubs off onto the customer. On the other hand, we are both honest and can't rave about a book we don't really like. In that case we comment upon the content or the author and refrain from giving our own opinion. Customers soon know whether or not you are making a recommendation with integrity and the same applies to the French publishers and translators. Some want advice and some don't – if it's the latter, we leave them alone to browse.

Some of the visitors stumble upon the Australian Bookshop by chance. A young man strolls into the shop one weekend, surprised to find an Australian bookshop on the banks of the Seine. He introduces himself as Scott Hillier and tells Claire and I that he is an Australian combat cameraman. As all Australians seem to do when they meet another Australian in Europe, we ask where he is from.

He smiles and says, 'Oh, I'm sure you wouldn't know the place. It's in outback Queensland.'

'Tell us anyway,' I say, and he tells us that he comes from Cunnamulla. 'Yes,' I say, 'here it is,' and point to the map of the region given to us by Herb Wharton. It's hanging on the wall, a few inches from Scott's head and there is a big red circle around Cunnamulla. Herb also left us some tourist brochures so we give one to Scott and a few weeks later I receive a letter from Herb containing a newspaper clipping from the local Cunnamulla newspaper, *The Western Sun*, describing the incident and Scott's astonishment at finding Cunnamulla being promoted on the Left Bank of Paris.

Not long afterwards another photographer enters the bookshop carrying a poster of Melbourne city's doorways. There are many lovely old buildings in central Melbourne and Tony Lucas has photographed some of their entrances. It's a stunning poster, full of memories for me, because I lived for a long time in Melbourne before migrating to Sydney and thence to Paris.

Of course we ask Tony where he's from and we receive almost the same answer as before: 'Oh, you won't have heard of it. It's just a small town in the Western District of Victoria.'

I grin and say, 'Just try me!'

'I come from Macarthur,' said Tony and I laugh because I lived in nearby Hamilton for twelve years and taught a large number of students, many of whom came from the surrounding communities, including Macarthur. Tony and I become firm friends and discover that we have much in common, including a love of jazz and, *bien sûr*, France and the French language.

Another surprise visitor is a university lecturer from California, who walks past one day and, seeing some children's books in the window, asks whether we have any others. Thanks to Glenda we have a great selection. He is delighted and leaves the shop with a big box of Australian children's books to add to his university's collection of children's literature. He tells us that until today Australian children's books were not represented in the collection, so he is very pleased with his purchases, as am I.

We are beginning to realise just how large and untapped is the world market for Australian books. As well as interest from the US, we have received visitors from some of the Pacific islands, which are actually closer to Australia than to Europe, but these people are visiting Paris where they can see and handle the books so are happy to buy their books here. Ordering the right books from Australia is very important – we have to try to anticipate our various customers' needs and, of course, we can't send them back.

As expected, the Australian Bookshop becomes a mini tourist bureau and as well as asking for maps and tourist guides, most of the French want advice. One weekend a French conductor comes in and tells us that he is going to conduct at the Sydney Opera House and then he thinks he will drive his wife and two small children to Cairns.

'How many days do you have for the trip?' I ask and he seems surprised.

'Two or three days.'

I take out a map and say that if he has such limited time it might be better to fly to Cairns. 'It's a very long car-trip for small children,' I add.

It is extremely difficult for people living in the smaller countries of Europe to imagine the huge distances in Australia, so we find a postcard with a map of Europe superimposed upon a map of Australia and this is helpful when we are called upon for tourist information. This happens at least once a day because there is no Australian tourism office in Paris and French tourists are instructed to phone London, which for various reasons they are loath to do. They much prefer to come to the Australian Bookshop, look at the books and chatter to us. We have already received a few postcards from them and so far there is only one person who hasn't been satisfied with her trip to Australia. She wrote to say that she had flown from Perth to Adelaide to Melbourne to Sydney to Cairns and back to Sydney in ten days. As she must have spent most of the time in the air it is little wonder that she didn't enjoy her holiday.

By November we are beginning to receive many orders from academics and students in Germany, Italy, Spain and Switzerland, as well as France. The European publicity has been good and word-of-mouth has also helped. Sometimes the academic orders are difficult and time-consuming, especially when they want books that are out of print or hard to find, but I do my best.

The students often have no idea what they need so Claire and I draw up lists of suggested reading for various topics. Sometimes the Australian Bookshop seems like a continuation of my secondary and tertiary teaching careers and, of course, Claire has just completed her *doctorat* so is familiar with the French system. I think we make a good team.

Towards the end of October a young Australian man called John walks into the bookshop – we chat for a while and then he offers to help me every Friday. This is like a gift from the gods because not only is he doing a *doctorat* on French cinema but he has experience in the world of finance. (He is a mature-age student who previously worked in banking.) We quickly become good friends and he gets on well with everyone – that is, unless some sort of bureaucratic bungle occurs and then he is very good at putting things right. His determination is one of his strongest features.

During these early days I receive an order from the Australian Embassy. It is gracious of them to give me the order because, I suppose, they would normally use the diplomatic bags. They ask for a quote but insist that my prices must be no higher than those of the Co-op Bookshop in Sydney. I oblige of course, although I cannot cover costs. For a start, the Co-op is able to give a discount to everyone who registers with them and, secondly, an Embassy can probably avoid customs and TVA. I can't!

Many French translators and publishers come in to introduce themselves and search for books. The first of these is Marc de Gouvenain of Actes Sud, who asks us to suggest some Australian books that might appeal to the French. Claire and I recommend several and Marc leaves the shop with seven under his arm.

A couple of days later Marc phones to tell us that he is so excited about one of the books, *Night Surfing* by Fiona Capp, that he has already bought the rights. We are thrilled because we hadn't expected such a quick decision. Normally, I am sure, it would take much longer but the timing just now is right because this year, following a visit to Australia, Marc founded *Antipodes*, a series of books featuring Australian writers, for Actes Sud.

He has already been successful at introducing Scandinavian literature to the French and hopes to do the same with Australian literature. Marc believes that by regularly publishing Australian authors he will build up a public for them just as he has done with the Scandinavians. In 1997 he was planning to publish two New Zealand and two Australian books: Alan Duff's *Once Were Warriors*, Elspeth Sandys' *Finding Out*, Liam Davison's *The White Woman* and John Bryson's *Evil Angels*. Now in October the same year he plans also to publish Fiona Capp's *Night Surfing* and the year after that he will publish Susan Johnson's *Flying Lessons*, Alan Duff's *One Night Out Stealing* and Liam Davison's *Soundings*.

Marc aims to publish a dazzling, eclectic selection of authors, chosen mainly because he himself enjoys their books so wants to read more of their work. He has been quoted as saying that he finds the 'relationship between man and the environment particularly appealing in Australian writing' and it would seem he is drawn to settings that are vastly different from French landscapes.

⤬ ⤬

The November *rencontre* will be the first *salon littéraire* organised without Glenda's help and I am anxious for it to succeed. Claire is very helpful too, and the Embassy sends out the invitations via their mailbag. Australian writer and poet Thomas Shapcott will be our guest and we invite him to talk about Australian literature at home and abroad as well as presenting some of his own writing. He has just received a special prize acknowledging his contribution to Australian literature and he is still executive director of the National Book Council and administrator of the Translation Grants Programme, so he has an enormous amount to offer by way of his experiences. The evening goes well – Tom is encouraging and inspirational and there is a lot of interest from the French, especially regarding translation. He also gives me some practical advice, as he knows the French publishing community well.

By now I realise there are many other Australians who have lived in Paris for a long time and are so well integrated that they no longer feel the need to seek out other

Australian expats. They call in, now and then, to tell me about themselves but rarely buy a book and don't seem to be interested in the *rencontres*. One of them calls in to inform me quite bluntly that there are 'no good Australian novels anyway'. I respect her wish to remain outside Australian contemporary culture and don't invite her to our soirées.

Sallyanne Atkinson gives me the phone number of an expat she thinks I should meet so I phone him and we arrange to meet on the terrace of the pâtisserie Dalloyau, opposite the Jardins de Luxembourg at 2 Place Edmond Rostand. Anthony Fowler is a lecturer in international law at the Sorbonne and great fun to be with as he is very charming, knows lots of people and is an entertaining raconteur. After some excellent coffee and one of Dalloyau's famously delicious *pâtisseries*, we decide to stroll in the Luxembourg gardens, already one of my favourite places in Paris.

The gardens are a calm oasis in the middle of this busy city and as we enter from Boulevard Saint-Michel, the orderly rows of chestnut trees with raked gravel paths below, the multitude of carefully tended flowerbeds and the rows and rows of metal chairs invite us to rest a while. Normally I would accept the invitation and go no further.

Today we keep walking – for those who enjoy activity, these quiet pathways lead to the Grand Bassin (a large lake) in front of Marie de Medici's Palais de Luxembourg.

Children sail boats on the lake but I'm told they aren't allowed to bring their own – they must hire them here. The gardens cover twenty-three hectares and are full of surprises – we discover sweeping lawns with a variety of trees and statues, an orchard, tennis courts and for the children a playground, pony-rides and the celebrated *marionnettes du Luxembourg*. Further on is another oasis – the English garden with its winding paths and collection of beautiful trees from all over the world, including a giant sequoia near the entry from rue August Comte. Here we decide to rest a while.

When I later visit Anthony at his apartment near the Seine I discover that he has one of the most wonderful views in Paris, framed by a wide corner window of his *salon*. You enter the room and there before you is the Seine and the back of Notre Dame. In the evening, with the flood-lights reflected in the water and the lights of the *bateaux-mouches* sweeping across them, Notre Dame's flying buttresses look as though they really are swirling off into the powdery blue and golden sky. It's a superb view and living there must be like living with a beautiful painting. My host opens a bottle of good champagne and soon I am in heaven.

Anthony is relaxed and gregarious so can be relied upon to help out in an emergency. One day a woman from a Paris TV station arrives at the shop and says that she desperately needs an anchorman for a lifestyle show. They have decided that Australia is to be the theme of the show and she asks whether I know an Australian who speaks French and has the presence to do the job.

'I know someone who would be perfect,' I say, and add, '*En plus, il est beau!*' (He's also good-looking.)

I phone Anthony and persuade him that he will have fun being the token Australian on a French travel show. All goes well until they ask him about Australian cuisine. As he hasn't lived in Australia for quite some time he phones me and asks, 'What do Australians cook these days?'

I answer that my friends and I prepare different kinds of Asian stir-fry dishes perhaps three times a week and then there is the traditional roast lamb and perhaps barbecued steak and fish. It's hard to generalise but this seems representative of the people I know. Anthony acquits himself very well at the recording of the show but three days later he rings, in a panic.

'Elaine, they want to print an Australian stir-fry recipe on the show's website and I have no idea what to tell them.'

'Don't worry,' I say, 'Claire and I will come up with something.'

To begin with, I invent a stir-fry recipe with Asian vegetables and fish and write it out in English. Then we begin translating, which takes some time because we have to keep phoning Claire's mother to find the French names for the fish, the measurements and the vegetables. In the end we come up with quite a good recipe which is posted on the website under Anthony's name. If we weren't so busy I would ask him to cook it for us!

One day Anthony introduces me to a young Frenchman called Stéphane Jacob, who studied art in Paris before going to live in Sydney for a while. Until then, Stéphane tells me, he had never been confronted with Australian culture of any kind. Later he spent a year travelling and working in Australia and met many people connected with Australian art who introduced him to institutions, private collections and galleries. It was during this second trip that he met Isabelle de Beaumont, who became his business partner, and together they created Arts d'Australie – Stéphane Jacob in order to promote and sell Australian art.

Stéphane is charming and he soon becomes both friend and colleague as we decide to work together. In December we organise an exhibition of Aboriginal paintings at the Australian Bookshop. It's a simple affair, with the paintings stacked in order in the back room and Stéphane's mother, Liliane, passing them through one by one to the interior of the bookshop. Stéphane then explains the paintings to the guests, who are mainly French. He knows the paintings well and this knowledge, combined with his enthusiasm and his integrity, results in a wonderfully satisfying evening for all concerned. People are now very keen to look at the art books we stock and to learn more about Australian art. Although Stéphane deals with both Aboriginal and non-Aboriginal art, the people here tonight are clearly more fascinated with the Aboriginal paintings, especially those of Emily Kngwarreye.

I see my first 'Emily', *Yam Dreaming*, at the Australian Bookshop – it's a large stunning work, full of movement and colour, with swirling ribbons of rose pink, pale pink, white and orange, derived, Stéphane tells us, from the growth patterns of the yam, a tribal symbol of the life force. It is so alive and celebratory that it has a powerful effect upon me. Until now I've only seen Kngwarreye paintings in books. The immediacy of the original work has an impact that is similar to the shocked reaction I felt at seeing my first real Impressionist paintings when they were still gathered together in the intimacy of the Jeu de Paume – the colours seemed so vibrant and alive in comparison with the colours in even the best-produced art books. It is winter now and Paris looks cold and grey, almost monochromatic, in direct contrast with the bold colours of these paintings that evoke the strong sunshine and the harsher colours of the Australian environment.

Stéphane and I decide to send out joint Christmas/New Year cards and we seek permission to copy one of the Indigenous Australian paintings that he is showing in Europe. Permission is received, royalties are paid and thousands of our cards go around the world with both of our names on them – the web's spreading wider in just a few months. I think ours will be a good collaboration.

I am really lucky that Bernard Cohen is the resident Australian writer at the Cité des Arts during these early days in the life of the Australian Bookshop because he and Nicola are very supportive and experience some of the growing pains with me, including an unforgettable *soirée littéraire* organised for us by the self-styled Dr Matilda X.

The story begins like a fairy tale, on a chilly December morning, when a very high-powered and glamorous African-American woman sweeps into the shop. She tells me she is passionate about New World writing and for a long time has 'really wanted to help Australian writers to become better-known'. She gives me her card and I see she has an important position with a long-established American institution in Paris, so I do not doubt her credibility. She says that she would like to organise a soirée for an Australian writer at Gallerie Toft, a large French art gallery further along the quai. She will invite lots of Americans and will also take care of the catering and drinks. I will not have to do anything!

As Bernard is still in Paris, I ask him whether he is interested and then give him her contact number so she can talk with him about the arrangements and the payment for his appearance. It all seems too good to be true – she tells me that I don't need to invite my friends, as she will introduce a whole new audience to Australian writing. She is very upbeat but, for some reason, I feel cautious, so take her at her word and only invite a handful of my customers. Anyway, the *rencontres* at the Australian Bookshop are free of charge whereas Matilda's evening is quite expensive and I don't want to upset those who, I hope, will become my regular guests. I reason to myself that I don't really need to invite my customers, because Matilda repeatedly assures us that dozens of Americans will be coming.

I am quite excited as the evening draws near. It's a wonderful venue, hordes of people are coming and I have absolutely nothing to do and no expenses. But when I arrive at the gallery I find Bernard and his family, my few close friends, the owners of the gallery and . . . Matilda. No Americans. It's a big disappointment but Bernard is philosophical and we have a pleasant evening. The next day I phone her workplace and discover that Matilda was sacked a few days previously because they checked her credentials and discovered that she had a history of gaining money through confidence trickery. I suppose she thought that a lot of people would come and that she would make a tidy profit from the evening as the space was free and her catering was minimal.

Bernard tells me that as payment from Matilda he received a cheque drawn on an Indonesian bank, which he is going to frame and hang on his wall. I am very lucky that

I didn't send out the 150 invitations I normally would have done for a *rencontre* at the Bookshop and I am also lucky that Bernard was the Australian author involved in Matilda's little scam. Others might not have been amused.

❧ ❧

The Australian Bookshop has already developed its own special atmosphere, which customers say is relaxed and warmly inviting, and people seem to enjoy coming here. French author Christophe Bourseiller writes of the Australian Bookshop in his *Guide de l'autre Paris* that people feel 'strangely transported in this unique place'. The French is much more elegant: '*On se sent curieusement dépaysé, dans ce lieu anglo-saxon à nul autre pareil.*'

Chapter 12

OF SATELLITES AND LYREBIRDS

'I cherished Elaine's shop. It was a place of pilgrimage for anyone in Paris who's passionate about Australian writing. As an Aussie stranded in London, it's still surprisingly hard to get a lot of Antipodean books in English book stores. But Elaine often stocked them. Her shop was in an iconic position and just going there lifted my heart – it was on Paris's left bank, right opposite the Seine, near Shakespeare & Co; an area still echoing with the ghosts of Hemingway, Stein, Sartre, de Beauvoir.'

Nikki Gemmell

PARIS, 1996

During these first few months in the life of the Australian Bookshop we are busy forging a place for ourselves in the Paris community and discovering who will turn out to be our major customers. Although a number of the Australian expats have become faithful customers and, in some cases, good friends, it is clear that they aren't our major market.

Nor are the Americans. There is, and has been, a large American expat presence in Paris ever since travel became possible for the average person, so there is the American Church, the American Library, Brentano's American Bookshop, WICE, the Thanksgiving Shop, various theatrical groups, magazines and a strong, recognisable American-in-Paris image which seems, in many ways, distinct from *la vie parisienne* itself. Even some of the literary landmarks, like Café de Flore and Les Deux Magots appear to me to have become somewhat Americanised and, of course, there are always American jazz musicians either visiting or living in France. Americans are obviously content and at home in *their* Paris, and few visit the Australian Bookshop.

The Americans who do come into the shop are usually tourists and they are often looking for Shakespeare & Company, the bookshop on the other side of Saint-Michel founded in 1951 by George Whitman and named after Sylvia Beach's original Shakespeare & Company, which was a lending library and bookshop in rue Odéon. It closed abruptly in 1941 when a Nazi officer wanted to buy Beach's only copy of *Finnegan's Wake* and threatened to confiscate her whole stock when she refused to sell it to him. The officer left, saying that he would return, and while he was gone Sylvia, her friend Adrienne Monnier and two others carried the entire contents of the shop up to an empty apartment on the fourth floor. Sylvia called in a carpenter to take down the shelves and a painter to obliterate the name of the shop on the building. Her dream was over in two hours.

I've always loved the Sylvia Beach story – her initiative, her courage in first publishing James Joyce's *Ulysses* and then staying on in France during World War II have become part of Paris mythology. For this reason, hordes of young Americans (and Australians) flock to George's picturesque namesake bookshop in rue de la Bûcherie, which he tells me he bought for the proverbial 'song' in 1951. Many of these visitors are in love with the dream of Paris between the two World Wars and have ideas of reliving it through Shakespeare & Company – they are certainly not interested in the little antipodean bookshop down the road.

So, as expected, our main market is the French themselves and the most visible of these are the members of the satellites, some of whom I met during my market research year. They are the French lovers of Australia, whose *raison d'être* is to promote interest in their chosen country while trying to earn a living at the same time. Paris is full of these passionate *associations* working to promote their special objectives and a number of these are related to Australia, which, chiefly because of its distance from Europe, has long been regarded as exotic by the French.

Most of these 'Australian' *associations* revolve around the Australian Embassy, which is why I think of them as satellites. In some ways, some *associations* are more like fireworks displays than satellites – they are visible for a while, then they fragment, reload and off they go again in all directions. The more positive *associations* work steadily and complement the work of the Embassy's cultural and information officers.

Some of these Australia-orientated, non-profit-making associations in France include ABIE (Australian Business in Europe), AFA (Association France–Australie), Antipodes AFA, Eurostralia, ACFA (Association Culturelle Franco–Australienne), La Petite Maison, La Pérouse Boomerang Club de France, Vent du Rêve (Musique de Didgeridoo), France Australie (in Île de France, Saint-Martin de Ré, Villers-Bretonneux, Aix-Subiaco), Harmonic Fusion (Sound of Didgeridoo), D'Oz à Oz, Australia Provence Forever, Australia-sur-Loire, Cinéma des Antipodes, Cinq

Planètes (musique aborigène), Médiathèque des Trois Mondes, and Association des Gourmets d'Australie Périgord et Europe.

Many of these groups seem reluctant to collaborate, while others are friendly and anxious to participate in the adventures of the Australian Bookshop. A few are openly antagonistic but I'm still feeling joyfully optimistic and confident that I can operate independently of them all while still involving them. As an independent Australian bookshop, I shouldn't be affected by their competitiveness, which seems to have its origins in past events.

But the satellites are not as easy to manage as I thought. Some are fiercely competitive with other groups, and it seems that no sooner have I accepted the offer of help from one *association*, than another person or *association* warns me that they are not to be trusted. I try to ignore such comments but it is disconcerting, especially when they attack people who have become close to me. There are several trivial incidents but it is the accumulation of their petty bickering that becomes wearing.

A respected French translator who has travelled to Australia under the auspices of the Australia Council warns me that it will be 'very damaging' if I work with a certain group. She suggests forming a Reading Committee to choose and present new books that we recommend for translation to publishers; the group would comprise her, me and another Australian woman working in France. I say that I think it is a good idea but I just don't have the time to take on any more work at present. I consider her warning but dismiss it because there's little I can do about it, anyway.

A young French woman who has a shop selling Australian goods comes in one day to protest that *she* sells books and considers herself the centre for Australian culture in Paris. I tell her that the Australian Bookshop is not a cultural centre, just a small bookshop with a space for visiting artists to present their work. She is indignant and I have to pretend that I can't understand French when some of her friends comment loudly that Lionel's furnishings are *moche* (ugly). I am aware that some people just like stirring the pot so on occasions like this I pretend not to understand what is said.

But there is a funny side to the satellites' disputes: on a prominent shelf just below the counter we display two competing small Australian magazines, published by French satellites, and we often see them being rearranged by their editors so that the 'enemy's' magazine is hidden.

The two French businesswomen, who have taken it upon themselves to assist me, warn me about just about everyone else, which I suppose is significant, but I ignore them as best I can. It's unexpected and irritating, especially in these very early days. Perhaps the excessively passionate games they play are simply part of the French love of drama, but I can't

174

help feeling that a lot of time and energy is wasted this way and that it would be more beneficial for them and for Australia if they could only learn to collaborate. French friends tell me some horror stories about the brutality of business competition here in Paris and I realise that it is because these *associations* are actually small, non-profit-making businesses, in many cases struggling to survive. I understand now that the people running them *can* earn a living – people can be paid as long as the final *bilan* (balance sheet) for the year does not show a profit. I also now understand why Australian Cultural Attaché Angus MacKenzie said at the Australian Bookshop's opening party that it was a pity I could not create an *association*. The realisation of the extent of the competitiveness of the *associations* could be overwhelming but at the beginning, with the calm and practical support of Claire and Glenda, I smile at them all and forge ahead with the job of creating my small independent bookshop, with the emphasis on the word 'independent'.

Fortunately there are also some permanent and more positive satellites, such as ABIE, Arts d'Australie and the *associations* created by Jean-Paul and Monique Delamotte, who are ardent devotees of Australia. All of the books published by their *association* La Petite Maison are on sale in the Australian Bookshop. *Coonardoo*, in particular, is very popular and we've already sold many copies. Because La Petite Maison is a small press, problems of distribution make the dispersal of their books more difficult than for mainstream publishing companies but Jean-Paul works hard at trying to make them known throughout France.

Since the Australian Bookshop opened, Monique and Jean-Paul have been staunch supporters and Jean-Paul often presents our guest speakers. He has also introduced me to the dozen or so Parisian members of his *associations*, to the editor of a literary magazine and to the owner of the much-loved bookshop The Village Voice. In their enthusiasm, the Delamottes have created no less than four different non-profit *associations* – L'Association Culturelle Franco–Australienne in 1980 (ACFA); La Petite Maison in 1986; Ici Aussie in 1990 (a studio at Boulogne-Billancourt, which is rented to Australian artists and academics); and, in 1995, L'Atelier Littéraire Franco–Australien (ALFA).

Jean-Paul also co-founded the Association France-Australie (AFA) and was vice-president from 1983–1985. He has written many articles and papers on Australian culture and has translated Australian writers such as Marcus Clarke, Katharine Susannah Pritchard (*Coonardoo*, with Hélène Jaccomard), Geoffrey Dutton (*Et Voilà*), Frank Moorhouse, Maurillia Meehan, John Rowland, Tom Thompson, William La Ganza, David Malouf (*Untold Tales*), Chris Andrews and Paul Wenz.

When Glenda and David left at the end of October, Monique offered to help at the Australian Bookshop every

Thursday. This seems to be working well so far, although I feel she is concentrating mostly on selling the books of La Petite Maison and she doesn't think I try hard enough to sell their books. I've explained that I am here to promote as wide a variety of Australian writers as possible but our aims are different so we can only try to complement each other.

With Claire, John and Monique, I concentrate on our new customers. As well as members of the satellite groups there are many academics and other private individuals, some of whom have worked for years to promote Australian culture in France and they are always very keen to know about the latest books, as well as wanting to buy books that are out of print. Many soon become regular customers and some have become friends, so I queue up with the *bouquinistes* and register myself as a second-hand book dealer in order to be able to supply them with the books they need. From the police station in the 6th arrondissement I receive a Police Book in which all second-hand purchases must be registered.

Computers are not yet used very much in France. My theory is that this is because the French had the free use of Minitel for many years before the advent of personal computers. Minitel is a small computer that can be obtained, free of charge, from the Post Office and used at home to look up addresses, timetables and a host of other things. However, it's not connected to the Internet so can't be used in the same way as a personal computer. Fortunately the Australian Bookshop is connected to the Internet – it is a useful tool.

I am astounded to find advanced university students in France who don't own a computer. This lack of access to computers makes the role of the Australian Bookshop especially important to French students and academics, who have no easy way of learning about new Australian books unless they have personal contacts in Australia. The *Australian Book Review* would be a useful guide for them but the cost of importing it to the Australian Bookshop is too high and many academics say they can't afford personal subscriptions, which are very expensive because of freight costs. We can access it through the Embassy but don't often have time as we must go there during working hours.

It is a joy to deal with the students and academics. They tell me they love coming to the bookshop because they can see the new books, handle them, talk about them and decide which ones they want to buy. I am beginning to think that many European students know more about our Australian writers than does the average Australian student. Not as much Australian literature seems to be taught in Australian universities these days! In general the emphasis seems to be on creative writing courses.

One of the earliest promoters of Australian literature in France was Professor Victor Dupont at the University of

Toulouse, which has what is probably the most important public collection of Australian books in France. In 1968 Professor Dupont set up a postgraduate course on Commonwealth literature, the focus of which was essentially Australia and New Zealand. This project was supported by the Literature Board of the Australia Council, whose gifts of books established the core of the University's library of Australian books.

One of Dupont's students, Xavier Pons, has now enthusiastically taken over the Australian studies department at Toulouse; his many other activities include translations, publications and radio talks, articles in newspapers and participation in international Australian studies conferences. The Australia Council sponsored Xavier's first trip to Australia when he was working on his PhD, and while he was there he made contacts with Sydney University's Co-op Bookshop, which enabled him to get books more quickly.

He explains to me that in France, whenever a university buys anything from abroad, the goods must be delivered first and payment is made much later because the Bank of France must vet all transfers of funds. Not many suppliers are prepared to wait for six months before they get paid and they tended to lose interest in dealing with him.

For me this is also a problem and, of course, the costs of consolidating the books in Australia plus the costs of freight, customs duty, delivery and TVA mean that the prices of Australian books at my bookshop are much higher than they would be if bought directly from the Co-op.

Through the customers of the Australian Bookshop, I become aware of the teaching of all kinds of Australian studies in primary schools, secondary schools and universities in France and other European countries. I don't think this interest is widely enough acknowledged and exploited by the Australian Government, because these students often go on to become regular readers of Australian books and a substantial number of them visit Australia at some time in their lives. They thus become unofficial ambassadors and have realistic views of the Australian way of life – they know that it's not just beaches and red kangaroos. In this context, for more than thirty years, as well as buying quantities of books for their library, Toulouse University must surely have produced many lovers of Australian literature and the Australian way of living. It must also have been responsible for the dispersal of a large number of Australian books into France. Other universities which have nurtured unofficial Australian ambassadors include Nîmes, Paris IV, the Sorbonne, Le Havre, Paris 9, Rennes, La Rochelle and Valenciennes. So while prohibitive costs and local regulations may mean I can't supply books directly to the universities for their collections, I have no doubt that they are creating a loyal base of customers who love Australian literature.

The other customers I love are the collectors, especially the armchair travellers who collect every Australian book translated into French. One of my favourites is a woman called Patricia Le Dorlot, who tells me that she travels through the books. Like many people she loves the idea of the Australian landscape, especially the interior, with its red earth, road trains and never-ending horizons. She says that whenever she reads an Australian book she imagines she is there. Other collectors ask for more unusual books – I was stunned when someone asked for a book on collecting egg-cups, but I found it in a small Australian country town. I have also been asked for Bill Mollison's books on perma-culture, which seem to have found international fame and, of course, there are those who collect books on sharks, whales, bushrangers, mounted police, crime stories, AFL football . . .

ক্ষ৹ ৹ক্ষ

Christmas is approaching and the Australian Bookshop has been officially open for three months. So much has happened that I haven't even had time to think about choosing a logo for the bookshop, but the arrival of Adrian Cooke reminds me that this is something I really want to do. Adrian comes from Yarragon, a picturesque little town in Gippsland, Victoria, and he has been introduced to me by family friends. When he returns to Australia, he is going to study design so he offers to work on an Australian Bookshop logo. He says he can include the work in his portfolio so will do it free of charge.

The difficulty is that I'm not quite sure what I want. Adrian tries some abstract designs based on the name – they are very stylish but I decide that I want something that is distinctively Australian without being too much of a cliché. Then I remember a book I read in 1995, Jim Davidson's *Lyrebird Rising*, the story of Louise Hanson-Dyer and her Lyrebird Press. It would be fun to have a logo with an Australia-France literary connection, so I tell Adrian about this book.

Louise Hanson-Dyer, an eccentric Australian woman, established a publishing company in Paris in the thirties and called it Editions de l'Oiseau-Lyre (Lyrebird Press). To begin with she published editions of Early Music, faithful to the original manuscripts at a time when Early Music was often recomposed by its editors. Having published her editions, Louise Hanson-Dyer then went on to promotion and record production with original instruments. In fact, her company, L'Oiseau-Lyre, produced the first long-playing records to be made in France.

Before settling in Paris, Louise had tried living in England but did not feel at home there – she felt at home in Paris. Davidson comments that her eccentricities and Australian accent were probably much more acceptable to the French than the English. She was an exotic and interesting foreigner in France, whereas in the England of the day some may have regarded her as a 'colonial'. I wonder whether things have changed much.

Although L'Oiseau-Lyre was famous for its fine music publications and records, Hanson-Dyer also supported Australian writers and artists and publicised them in Paris at a time when there was no official Australian Ambassador. She first thought of using the platypus as a logo but, in the end, her registered logo (*marque*) became the lyrebird, which is probably just as well because *Editions de l'Ornithorynque* is quite a mouthful.

The lyrebird portrayed on the official registration form of L'Oiseau-Lyre is a rather sedate, more or less realistic-looking bird, but later books and records show beautiful, stylised creatures, some of them designed by Australian artist Sam Atyeo. I own a beautiful little L'Oiseau-Lyre edition of *Trois Chansons de Francois Couperin* with the cover design by Rose Adler – the elegantly swirling tail-feathers on the endpapers are exquisitely understated and very beautiful.

When she received an invitation to address the Australian Literature Society, Louise Hanson-Dyer decided that Australian authors should be better promoted in the rest of the world. She organised some literary competitions with generous prizes and promises of translations into French but although the prizes were awarded the scheme fell through, mainly, it seems, because she wanted to have the right to adapt or cut the books, rather than simply to translate them.

When I have finished telling him this story, Adrian too is convinced that we should also choose a lyrebird for the Australian Bookshop logo and he puts considerable effort into a variety of stylised designs. Suddenly Christmas is upon us and, before I know it, he and his folio have disappeared back home before any decision has been made.

I leave it for a while and then a French friend of David's, Julie Scobeltzine, offers to have a try. I've decided that I prefer something more realistic and somehow incorporating the name of the shop. I give Julie some postcards because, of course, she has never seen a lyrebird. The first image she shows me is attractive and the tail is beautiful but the legs are too short. She goes away and comes back with the version I now use – it is not a streamlined design, nor is it a really accurate depiction of a lyrebird, but it is charming and incorporates the words 'Australian Bookshop', in a circle which follows the curve of the bird's tail. Eventually it is registered in France as the *marque* (trademark) of the Australian Bookshop, ready to be featured on our planned website and on the stationery. Julie also plans to paint it on the front door but just now she is busy with theatre costume design, so the door must wait.

As Christmas Day draws near we are very busy but I find time to reflect upon the past twelve months. It's had its dramas, and dealing with French bureaucracy has been every bit as bad as people said it would be. Finding and renting the shop was complicated and time-consuming and even finding a shipping agent with offices at both ends was a Herculean task I could never have survived without the help of my children. Ginny has liaised endlessly with Melbourne shipping agents, Richard and Ginny have both taken care of my Sydney assets and David has supported me in Paris. The frustrations of dealing with the squabbling satellites have been totally eclipsed by the wonderful people, both customers and helpers, from all over the world, who have combined to establish the Australian Bookshop as a haven for Australians and a window into Europe for Australian books and writers.

Despite the occasional setback, 1996 has been a fantastic year for me. I've seen my dream come true and the opening of the bookshop has created a lot of interest, not only here in Paris but in other parts of Europe as well. The shop itself has become my home, because I spend more time here than anywhere else. I've always viewed bookshops as inviting treasure-houses, filled with all kinds of delights, so I count myself lucky to be living in one. I've met such a kaleido-scope of interesting and – for the most part – friendly people that I couldn't wish for more.

But I am mistaken – a wonderful Christmas gift arrives, just a little ahead of time, in the shape of my daughter,

Ginny, her husband and their two little boys. I am blessed and, even though I only close for one day to celebrate Christmas Day with them, it is one of the best memories of a very memorable year. My little grandsons, Ross and Harry, are three and six respectively and I will always remember their first visit to the bookshop. They immediately spot the children's shelves, just inside the front door, and they just stand there silently for a while, gazing, surprised and delighted at recognising old friends like Possum Magic and Blinky Bill in a bookshop on the other side of the world.

I rush for the camera and now treasure a photograph of them, two little chubby Australian boys, sitting on the floor, engrossed in one of their favourite books, quite oblivious of their surroundings and the miracle of being in the Australian Bookshop on the Left Bank in Paris.

Chapter 13

THE WEB WIDENS

'You created a place in Paris which became an intersection for two cultures so it attracted the most interesting people from both English- and French-speaking countries. There was a constant stream of visitors and I felt as though I was part of the Parisian life. . . . And being in that part of Paris was especially exciting – working in a bookshop on the Left Bank was something I hadn't even dreamt of doing.'

John Emerson

PARIS, 1997

By January the Australian Bookshop is well-established and playing an active part in both the French- and English-speaking Paris arts communities. There are always lots of volunteer helpers but Claire de Robespierre and John Emerson are the core assistants who can be relied upon to be there every week. John is in Paris researching French cinema for his PhD at Adelaide University, but he comes every Friday to help at the bookshop, which seems to have become a drop-in centre and a reference point for Australian culture in Paris.

My working days are long but I'm helping people and facilitating meetings between writers, translators, publishers, teachers, students and the general public, as well as publicising Australian culture. The feedback is good, I feel useful and enjoy the everyday experiences of life as a bookseller on the Left Bank.

This area is full of bookshops and publishing houses and I've visited most of them – during the renovations some booksellers came in and invited me to join a group of colleagues who regularly lunch together. Because I want to stay open during the lunch hour and because I envisaged being alone in the shop, I felt I had to refuse their invitation and still regret that I did so.

There's a tiny little French bookshop further along the quai, towards the Gare d'Orsay. The owner is a Frenchman called Vincent and he is a wonderful neighbour, very friendly and helpful. One day he comes rushing in to tell me that the owner of the card shop on the corner of rue Saint-André des Arts is renovating his store and all of his card-stands are sitting on the pavement waiting to be taken away. If I like, we can hurry around the corner and buy them at an 'interesting' price. An 'interesting' price means that they will be inexpensive and, as I have been planning to buy some new stands for the small books and postcards, I place a *fermée* sign on the door and hurry around the corner with Vincent. Soon afterwards, feeling very pleased with ourselves, we return to our bookshops with fine cardstands.

Near the church, Saint-Séverin, on the opposite side of Boulevard Saint-Michel, is a short street called rue de la Parcheminerie and in this street is the Abbey Bookshop, which sells new and second-hand books in English. Owner Brian Spence is Canadian, so his speciality is promoting Canadian books and writers, but he is interested in other countries and has received a number of Australian writers as guests at his soirées in the beautiful mediaeval *cave* below his shop. Brian is a charming host and speaks eloquently in both French and English. I join him and his friends on the Pont des Arts to celebrate Canada Day. How I wish

Australia Day weren't in the middle of winter – the Pont des Arts is such a romantic setting for a party.

In the mornings I usually leave home at about 7.30 and stop at one of the bistros on the Place Saint-André des Arts for *un café* (short black) at the counter with the workmen. (There are usually three prices for drinks here in Paris, the least expensive being the drink taken standing at the counter and the most expensive the leisurely drink on the *terrasse*.) I sometimes ask for a *tartine* (fresh buttered baguette) but mostly I don't eat breakfast.

When the market opens in nearby rue de Buci, I close the shop and rush down there to buy provisions. I love the hustle and bustle and the smells of French markets – you can't possibly buy everything but it's great to window-shop and gaze at the huge variety of breads, cheeses, sausages, mushrooms, *pâtés* and *terrines*, fruit and vegetables. I never cease to marvel at the efficient way the providores are able to supply fresh produce daily; they must get up before dawn. And they always know where the food (and wine) comes from, saying that the flavour is related to the *terroir* (the soil). I wish I had all day to stay and drink in the atmosphere.

On the way back to the shop I pass extraordinary *pâtis-series* and *traiteurs* (caterers), where the simplest cakes, pastries and savoury delicacies are all beautifully presented; even the *oeuf gelé* (jellied egg) is an enticing little artwork.

There's a very good florist as well, and I sometimes buy wattle (*mimosa*) and gumtips to add their distinctive perfumes to the atmosphere of the bookshop.

I love the *rencontres* and enjoy meeting the Australian writers but it is also very satisfying when the Australian Bookshop gradually becomes involved with Parisian cultural and theatrical groups, including Moving Parts, which meets at the bookshop every second Sunday. Gradually we are building close relationships with French translators and publishers as well as with readers. This is perhaps the most rewarding part of my work.

We decide to celebrate the beginning of 1997 with a rollicking, good-humoured evening centred around the book *Smashed*. *Smashed* is an anthology of Australian drinking stories, edited by Matthew Condon and Richard Lawson. It includes stories by Henry Lawson, Carmel Bird, Rosie Scott, Frank Moorhouse, Mandy Sayer and David Ireland.

Having discovered that three of the contributors will be in Paris at the same time, it seems a good idea to invite them to read their stories from this collection. José Borghino, Tim Baker and Venero Armanno entertain us by reading their short stories and, as the shop has only been officially open for five months, there is a great deal of interest and curiosity, especially from the French. I'm not sure whether they expect good writing or something else but it's a very relaxed evening and everyone seems happy.

And happy they should be – in keeping with the theme
of the book we have consumed every drop of Vinnie's wine
and some of us are ready for 'the plains that we all ride
across after a few too many . . . The different landscapes we
visit whilst drunk'. (I quote from the book's publicity blurb.)
Atypically, this evening's *rencontre* was not bilingual, so
I'm uncertain of just how much our French friends have
understood. They certainly understand the atmosphere of
merriment and join in the fun.

We repair to La Tourelle, the little restaurant in rue
Hautefeuille which I discovered many years ago when I first
visited David and one of his friends lived in the house
behind. It is run by two sternly professional Frenchwomen
of a certain age. Their little dog sits in a basket on the
counter. The low ceiling of this mediaeval building is covered
with mirrors and there are lots of colourful old theatre and
book posters on the far wall. It's crowded, the toilets are in
the interior courtyard and sometimes the service is unsmil-
ing because the owners seem to hire smart, professional
young women of a similar ilk to themselves, but they don't
mind if the party becomes a little rowdy; in fact, they seem
to enjoy it. The food is what the French would call 'good
honest food' and they serve *escargots, bourguignon, andouil-
lette* (very smelly) and other such traditional French dishes
(*les plats de grandmère*). As well, the *pichets* of wine are not
expensive – it's the perfect spot for continuing our *Smashed*

rencontre. Tonight the service is stunning because Venny Armanno has charmed our *serveuse* (waitress) – it seems to be a case of love at first sight and she can't do enough for us.

The American newspaper *Paris Free Voice* features *Smashed* on its books page. The headline reads 'New Aussie bookshop . . . it's a smash'. The article mentions the fact that expat Tim Baker's story, 'L'Absinthe', is an extract from his novel which is set mainly in Picasso's old studio on the rue des Grands Augustins, just around the corner from the Australian Bookshop. Every corner of Paris has a story attached to it and as I become aware of these stories, places become more significant and influence the way I feel about the city. The Australian Bookshop's special corner of Paris, the Quai des Grands Augustins, is the oldest quai (riverside road/embankment) in Paris and was built in 1313 so that King Philip the Fair would not get muddy as he travelled from his palace (le Palais de la Cité) to his mansion (l' Hôtel de Nesle). J.G. Ballard has witten: 'We live inside an enormous novel.' In Paris, I think, I live inside a vibrant, multi-layered, multi-media theatrical production where the past is just as present as whatever it is we are trying to create today. It's exciting to be part of it all!

Not long after the *Smashed* evening I meet Jacques Rancourt, the director of the Franco-Anglais Festival of Poetry. He asks me if I would like to assist with the Festival in May this year. He has already invited an Australian guest, poet Vivian Smith, whose poetry I have always admired, so I willingly agree. Jacques explains that the Festival commenced in 1977 with the idea of broadening communication between poets speaking different languages. As this is also one of the main aims of the Australian Bookshop I am delighted to be involved. The ensuing poetry festival is, for me, a highlight of the year.

In addition to organising round-table conferences and translation workshops, and publishing *La Traductière* (a magazine containing poems, cross-translations and articles relating to the art of translation), the Franco-Anglais Festival of Poetry presents readings. In 1997, fifty-three poets from thirteen countries participate. As the Festival draws near I discover that at least three other fine Australian poets will be in Paris during the month of May so suggest to Jacques that I hold an 'umbrella event' in conjunction with the Festival. He has never heard this term but, when I explain what it means, he agrees and develops the idea further to include readings at a number of other venues such as the Abbey Bookshop, Tea and Tattered Pages, Les Cahiers de Colette, Tigh Johnny's – The Irish Pub, Librairie à Tire d'Aile and Shakespeare & Co.

Participating Australian writers are Gary Catalano, Luke Davies, John Tranter and, of course, Vivian Smith, the official Australian guest who will work on the cross-translations with other official guests. All readings are free

194

and presented in French and English. At the Australian Bookshop *rencontre* it is great to hear the Australian poets reading alongside such French poets as Maryline Desbiolles, Yves Bichet, Anne Portugal and Gérard Noiret. It represents a step towards my long-held vision of meaningful cross-cultural exchange through poetry and literature.

This year is the Festival's twentieth anniversary, so there is a special closing concert in the beautiful little Théâtre Molière at La Maison de la Poésie (House of Poetry) in the Passage Molière, which runs between rue Quincampoix and 157 rue Saint-Martin, quite close to the *Centre Pompidou*. Jacques has invited painters, sculptors, photographers and musicians to create works inspired by the poetry and twelve musicians and actors contribute to a performance of the texts with music composed for the work of each of the twelve special guest poets. The artworks are on display during the festival at La Maison des Ecrivains.

This final concert is my first visit to the Maison de la Poésie, the concept of post-war French poet Pierre Seghers, who promoted a 'humane, living and communicable poetry'. The Maison de la Poésie was first situated at Les Halles but later moved to the Théâtre Molière, founded in 1791 as a public theatre to present plays of all kinds. The theatre itself has a fascinating history: when Napoleon decreed in 1807 that numerous French theatres were to be suppressed, it became a physical education hall, an army hall for concerts, banquets and the like. I am happy to see it restored to its former ornate glory and to see the whole complex dedicated to shows, readings, conferences and other events which seek to promote world poetry. There are two main spaces (both of which are intimate enough for poetry events) and some smaller rooms downstairs where poetry books are stored. These, too, can be used for workshops and meetings. I am entranced by the concept and at the acknowledgement of poetry by both the French Government and the Mairie de Paris (Paris Town Hall).

As a member of the Festival committee, I translate contrasting styles of poetry from France, Belgium and Quebec. Poetry translation is, for me, a wonderful way to explore the intricacies of French language and thought, and I am especially interested in the poetry from French-speaking countries outside France. I love words and I love the French language, so it is fascinating to see the variations in the use of the language by poets who come from Canada, Switzerland, Haiti and Belgium. Maybe it's because I'm an outsider too. I find translation work exhilarating and very rewarding. The poetry and translations resulting from the Franco-Anglais Festival of Poetry are published each year in a review, *La Traductière*, usually launched at the main festival.

As well as experiencing the pleasure of listening to the cross-translations, I am thrilled to be meeting like-minded members of the Parisian arts community and am honoured and delighted to be invited to share a *pôt* with them or, in the case of Jacques and his wife, Marie-France, to visit their home and share food, friends and conversation.

⸎ ⸎

Our web of customers is rapidly expanding and Claire, John and I enjoy selling books, talking to people and giving each potential buyer our personal attention and a cup of tea or coffee if they are so inclined. Most of those who enter the shop are curious and want to talk about Australia and ask questions about the books. French customers tell me this is very different from a visit to the average Parisian bookshop, where buying books can be simply a commercial exchange. The poetry books are becoming well-thumbed as there is usually someone sitting on my brown leather captain's chair, in our poet's corner, reading avidly.

Monique Delamotte continues to assist me every Thursday and she also makes a valuable contribution through her intimate knowledge of the writers she and Jean-Paul met in Australia while living there in the 1970s. My teaching and writing experience in the fields of Australian music, history, art and literature – along with John's and Claire's cinema studies – equip us to 'teach' the French about Australian writing, for most people tell us that they know very little and want to learn.

197

A number of visiting Australian authors have wryly commented that perhaps we should be doing the same thing in Australia and several have observed that there is a better range of Australian books here in this Parisian bookshop than is found in most non-specialist bookshops in Australia. Since the opening of the shop last year, we have had difficulty in finding Patrick White's books in English, even though most of them are available in French, so I have had to search for second-hand copies. I am told that they will soon be re-published in English but it is awkward and a little embarrassing having to explain to the French that there isn't much demand for them in Australia.

Travelling expats still often come in just for the 'Australian' atmosphere, but most rewarding for us are the large numbers of French and other European customers, who continue to contact us either in person or by mail and email. Because of them, sales begin to increase as anticipated in the business plan approved by the French Chamber of Commerce back in 1995.

A very important moment in the evolution of the Australian Bookshop is when Australian poet John Tranter suggests that we should apply for help from the Australia Council with the expenses related to the promotion of Australian writers in Europe. I am immensely cheered and very grateful when, after subsidising the *rencontres* for the first year myself, the Australia Council's Literature Board agrees to help with the programme for 1997-98. José Borghino, Gail Cork and their team are very supportive of the bookshop's proposed promotional activities and a useful collaboration ensues.

The Australian Embassy in Paris keeps assisting with mail-outs of invitations, and Australian importer Vinnie Laing generously donates wine for most occasions. Michael Kennedy, owner of the first Australian pub in Paris, Café Oz in rue Saint-Jacques, helps with donations of wine and glasses. Otherwise, I'm on my own and obtaining books for readings at short notice is often expensive because I can't always wait for the books to come as a consolidated load through my shipping agent – for short-notice readings I have to order directly from the publishers and pay courier costs. It can sometimes be nerve-racking and on a couple of occasions the books arrive just a few hours before the *rencontre*. That, along with the French habit of arriving half an hour after the advertised time, still makes me anxious but I am gradually becoming more relaxed and tell myself that as long as the invited guest appears there is no cause for worry. On the other hand, it is desirable to be able to sell a few books on these occasions and it would be very embarrassing to have a poor turn-out, but so far my fears remain unfounded.

This year more and more French are coming into the Australian Bookshop to ask about travelling to Australia.

This is an interesting change because in the past they might have said 'too far away' or 'too much like America', whereas now we often hear, '*Oh, je rêve de l'Australie*' (I dream of Australia).

One young Frenchwoman arrives, in tears, to tell me that her application to emigrate to Australia has been refused. She married an Australian and was living with him in the Northern Territory where she worked as a kindergarten teacher. The marriage broke up and because she was no longer married to an Australian she was forced to return to France, where all she can do is dream about the life she loved on the other side of the world. She visits as often as possible 'just to soak up the atmosphere'. I visit the *école maternelle* where she works and teaches the children there about other children in Australia. The web widens.

We are discovering many more of the armchair travellers we identified last year as enthusiastic supporters of the Australian Bookshop. Some of them tell me they collect every Australian book published in French and that they love the Australian Bookshop for its atmosphere and because we make it so easy to find the Australian books in French.

These same armchair travellers love to go to the Etonnants Voyageurs festival at Saint-Malo. The Festival Etonnants Voyageurs (literally 'astonishing/wonderful/marvellous travellers') was created in 1989 by Michel

Le Bris and is an international literature festival devoted to travel writing. It attracts a huge crowd of approximately 50,000 visitors each year and has greatly increased sales of travel literature. In 1990, Michel Le Bris, Olivier Cohen and Alain Dugrand founded *Gulliver*, a magazine devoted to 'world fiction', and this too has been incredibly successful.

Each year at Etonnants Voyageurs Festival international du livre, to give it its full title, the Prix de l'Astrolabe Etonnants Voyageurs is awarded. This prize is donated by the travel bookshop Astrolabe and is given to a book in French which describes 'another world' in such an original way that it is an invitation to travel. A regular visitor to the Australian Bookshop, the affable Jacques Meunier, was founding president of the committee adjudicating this prize. He is a great travel writer and loves to recount tales of his adventures in his beloved Tasmania. I think one of the reasons for the success of this festival is that it is, for many, a doorway to the world outside France.

෴ ෴

Back at the Australian Bookshop orders are now coming in from countries other than France – Germany, Italy, Greece, Switzerland, England, the USA and even Uruguay. With the help of my friends at La Poste, I learn how to send boxes of books in postal bags at a more economic rate. Peter

Goldsworthy's book *Maestro* is popular in Switzerland because it is very well written and, importantly for younger teenagers, not too long. Another advantage is that the publishers have created a teaching aid in the form of a CD-rom to go with it. European teachers are very happy when publishers provide this kind of help.

Towards the end of the year, the French decide to add the topic 'The Republican debate in Australia from 1770 to the present day' to the Agrégation, which is a high-level university entrance exam. Fortunately Claire is able to help with new catalogues, listing available books about the Republican debate. And, once again, the gods smile upon me because Julie Burton, a young New Zealander, also offers to help us. Julie is a vivacious, intelligent and adventurous person, full of charm and good humour. The customers love her, and so do I, because she brings with her a practical intelligence plus extensive experience in sales and marketing.

John still comes in on Fridays, so although we are busy there is a happy work atmosphere and I feel really sad when Julie announces that she is moving on at the end of the year. Again, the gods are kind, because Australian artist Marion Borghelt introduces me to Raphaëlle Pomian, an artist and writer who has both Australian and French citizenship. A talented and intelligent woman, she lived in Melbourne for many years and now lives in Paris where she writes and

ЩЩ

ЩЩЩ

ЩЩЩ

ЩЩ ЩЩ

Щ Щ ЩЩ

Щ Щ

creates beautiful, ephemeral works in cigarette paper. Her work is mostly monochromatic and her use of textures and patterns, together with extraordinary effects of light and shade, results in works that are spiritual and uplifting. At the bookshop, Raphaëlle's insights into the cultural lives of both countries are invaluable and she becomes another important link in the chain of book-lovers who contribute to the development of the Australian Bookshop in Paris. Together we work on a little French/Australian phrase book for Assimil (language specialist publishers).

We have sold enough books now to know that Sally Morgan's *My Place* (called *Talahue* in French), Bruce Chatwin's *Songlines* (yes, I've told them he's not Australian), the Arthur Upfield books, Georges-Goulven Le Cam's *L'Australie et la Nouvelle Zélande* and Barbara Glowczewski's *Les rêveurs du désert* are among our best-sellers for the first twelve months. It is encouraging to note that, having read these books, customers usually return and ask about novels and other books. They seem particularly keen to know more about everyday life in Australia.

Ethnologist Barbara Glowczewski's book, *Les rêveurs du désert*, was written in French and appeals to those who want to know about Indigenous Australian traditions and culture. We have no hesitation in recommending it because Barbara has spent many years living with the Warlpiri people for long periods of time and the book is well researched.

Glowczewski wants to make a CD-rom about Warlpiri traditions, expressly for the Warlpiri themselves, so that these can be preserved and passed on to the younger generations. In ancient times this would have been done by word of mouth but because their lives are rapidly changing there is a danger that this might not continue.

A book we decide not to stock is Marlo Morgan's *Mutant Message Down Under* and I spend a lot of time explaining why it's not on sale at the Australian Bookshop. First published in the USA in 1994, it has since been translated into many different languages and is very popular with young people who tell me they find it inspiring, as well it may be. When I explain that Indigenous Australians dislike this book so much that some actually went to Japan, where the author was giving a lecture tour, to try to stop her, my customers seem surprised. They do not believe me when I say that she admitted that she had lied about the authenticity of the story and that the publisher then re-released the book as fiction. Finally I enlarge a newspaper article reporting these incidents and post it on the front door. A few weeks later, a couple of women stop in front of the shop and one of them stands on the top step, reading the article. When she is finished, she turns to her friend and says, 'Here's an article saying what a shitty book I've written.'

Then they continue on their way. It is the author herself

and I am serving a customer so miss the opportunity to talk with her.

One day a French publisher comes in and, after looking around the shop, asks why I don't stock Marlo Morgan's *Mutant Message Down Under*. Once again I explain that I cannot because I believe it is inaccurate and is considered insulting by the Aboriginal group whom she only visited for a few weeks and by Indigenous Australians in general. He is surprised and comments, in French, that this is not a 'commercial decision' on my part because the book is a bestseller in many countries. I reply that although I need eventually to make a profit, I have not opened the Australian Bookshop purely for financial reasons (I would not be so foolish) and that my main aim is to promote good Australian writing and facilitate intercultural exchange. I can't stock a book that I believe misappropriates another's culture, even if it is a bestseller. Lost for words, he departs.

Towards the end of this very full and satisfying year a small cloud looms on the horizon. The aftermath of an event which is, in many ways, a highlight in the story of the promotion of Australian books in France, becomes problematic for me. It begins when I received a message from the Information Officer at the Australian Embassy in Paris asking me to compile a list of twelve or more contemporary

Australian books which have been translated into French during the last twelve months. I'm told that I must include one travel and one art book. I do this and, after numerous conferences with the Cultural Officer as well as the Information Officer, the list is sent to television station France3, which is planning an Australian season in their series *Un livre un jour*.

The producer of the show, Rémy Lillet, comes to see me several times to discuss the show and I give willingly of my time. Filming is done in Australia with the support of the Australia Council and the Australia-France Foundation. It is a big publicity opportunity – two minutes for each book on twelve consecutive days at 6.30 pm, primetime, with an anticipated 3.2 million viewers per day and presented by well-known French TV personality, Olivier Barrot.

The books finally chosen from the original, slightly longer list are *Surfer la nuit* (Fiona Capp), *Dogfish* (Susan Geason), *Guide Australie* (Lonely Planet), *Pour l'amour d'une rose noire* (Nicholas Jose), *Un fils Australien* (Gordon Matthews), *Je me souviens de Babylone* (David Malouf), *La femme égarée* (Tim Winton), *Le chien de désert rouge* (John Bryson), *Peintres aborigines d'Australie* (ed. Sylvia Crossmann and Jean-Pierre Barou), *Talahue* (Sally Morgan), *L'agneau à l'abbatoir* (Jennifer Rowe) and *Crime au sommet* (Arthur Upfield).

Un livre un jour has previously filmed shows in Spain,

Germany and Japan but the Australian series is the largest yet and is a big hit. I attend the preview, held over breakfast at the Cercle de La Librairie, and I am impressed by the quality of the images. Members of the French media are also impressed and *Livres Hebdo* writes of the series' 'beautiful images, joyful rhythm and self-deprecating humour, along with [its] sound knowledge of contemporary Australian publishing in France'.

When my French friends hear of the hours I have spent working on this programme they are horrified and say, 'But you should have been paid a consultancy fee. *C'est normale!*'

I receive a charming thank-you letter from Rémy Lillet but there is no fee and no acknowledgement on the show itself. I am disappointed. The series should be a great boost for Australian books but it would have been even better if the viewers had been told that there is now an Australian bookshop in Paris where the books can be purchased in both French and English. I suspect that many of the French, including the people at France3, think the Australian Bookshop is a government organisation, and this is understandable, because most other countries have official Cultural Centres in Paris. It is a difficult problem because we all spend a large part of each day on tourism, preparing bibliographies, answering journalists' and translators' questions and performing other such services that are probably not offered in most bookshops. We can do this because the bookshop is not a formal cultural institution, remote from daily life and closed in the evenings and at weekends.

While an English magazine article last year described the bookshop as an Australian drop-in centre in Paris, I only wish that I had had a sufficiently large amount of money to have been able to really do something like that to promote Australian culture. But the fact is the French Chamber of Commerce has insisted that I must run a commercial bookshop if I am going to sell books. I cannot be a non-profit-making organisation if I am going to sell books. *C'est interdit!* The Australian Bookshop is a business and needs to sell enough books to begin making a profit at the end of three years. This is the target so I need as much help and publicity as possible. If it weren't for the positive feedback from satisified customers and the Parisian community I would be perturbed.

This conflict between the Australian Bookshop's image as a cultural/community centre and its reality as a business is reflected in the fact that I am not in close contact with Austrade as are other Australian businesses in Paris. Apparently I am considered to be under the cultural umbrella of the Embassy and, as the Cultural Officers do not seem to liaise with Austrade I seldom receive business information. It seems that the Australian Bookshop is a business but not a business. It's a confusing problem and seems insoluble.

⤛⟶ ⟵⤜

Television plays a large part in the general promotion of books in France. There are currently eleven shows a week concerning books, including *Nulle part ailleurs* (Nowhere Else), which is shown once a week on public television from 6.30 until 8.30 and has a considerable impact on sales. It's a talk show with entertainment and is very popular – although it's not exactly Oprah Winfrey, it is influential. If a book is mentioned or a writer is interviewed sales will soar. Bernard Pivot's *Bouillon de culture* (Culture Soup) is more specialised – it is a show that promotes books and reading. Publishers are very happy when Pivot mentions a book but friends tell me his previous show *Apostrophe* was even more popular than *Bouillon*. Pivot has also hosted a World French Spelling Competition – it was given the name *Les dicos d'or* (Golden Dictionaries) in 1993. Apparently in 1986 over a million viewers entered the competition. In 1998 the national finals of the *Dicos d'or* were held in the newly-built Stade de France. The next event held there was the Soccer World Cup. I read numerous articles paying tribute to Pivot's contribution to the promotion of literature through *Apostrophe*. Everyone agrees that it was a high point in the history of French television book programmes.

The *rencontres* presented during 1997 continue the celebratory theme begun with *Smashed* and cover an astonishingly diverse range of subjects including gardening with Holly Kerr Forsyth, the film industry with Steve Bisley, social history with Susan Mitchell, perfume with Michael Edwards and music with Peter Tahourdin.

Because of Marc de Gouvenain's speed in acquiring and then translating Fiona Capp's book, we were able to organise a *rencontre* for *Night Surfing* in English on 27 February and now a *lancement* of the French version on 6 November this year. The Australian Embassy also organises a small luncheon in honour of the French publication.

The launch of *Surfer la nuit* is a memorable evening, as are all of the *rencontres* we've held so far, but this one seems symbolic, full of goodwill and co-operation between the two cultures represented. The Australian Bookshop looks its best at night, with Daniel's rose-tinted lighting, and we have created one of our most striking window displays so far, using multiple copies of the book, with its distinctive sea-blue cover and the flesh-coloured profile of the surfer's face, plus some wonderfully atmospheric photographs of the sea by night. Fresh eucalyptus leaves found at the Marché de Buci give a faint odour of the Australian bush.

The *rencontre* is bilingual, because Marc introduces the book and reads a small section in French and Fiona follows with the same section in English. The floor is then open for questions and there is a stimulating discussion on translation. Because Fiona Capp has been in France this year while her book was being translated she has been able to collaborate with her translator and it's fascinating to be allowed to share a part of their experience. For me it's the beginning of what will become an enduring interest in translation. Until now, I haven't had time to read and compare the translations of Australian books into French (and vice versa) but I promise myself to do better in the future. I am usually content to ask native French speakers their opinions, but I vow to read more Australian books in French.

Marc de Gouvenain's visit to Australia has had a profound impression upon him and as a translator he responds to the landscapes in which the Australian books are set. He says that when he is translating a book he likes to read about the area and look at maps in order to imagine the setting and the atmosphere. Other representatives from Actes Sud are present at this wonderful *rencontre* and they seem happy to have the Australian Bookshop just around the corner from their Paris offices.

I have met a lot of other French translators of Australian books in the last twelve months and it is always interesting to ask how they were introduced to Australian literature. Well-known translator Françoise Cartano-Perrin said that for a long time she did not know much about Australian literature except for Patrick White, whom she thought of as European, and then she chanced upon the work of Peter Carey. She adds that this was before the days of '*Mad Max*', Werner Herzog,

Jane Campion and Bruce Chatwin'. Cartano then read *Just Relations* by Rodney Hall and was so impressed that she began not only to translate his works but also to read other Australian writers and, eventually, to travel to Australia.

After talking with many translators it seems that while Patrick White's winning of the Nobel prize was a breakthrough for Australian literature in Europe, Australian cinema is much better known in Europe than Australian literature. The cinema is obviously a gateway through which people can be introduced to writing but doing this requires a sound knowledge of both films and books. I become ever more grateful to have Claire and John helping at the Australian Bookshop; their combined expert knowledge of Australian cinema and books is a valuable resource.

Some of the translators who visit the Australian Bookshop are searching for new books to translate and others just want to chat or ask questions such as, 'What is a strawberry shake?'

'What's a Stobie pole?'

'How long is an echidna?'

A young man who is writing a thesis on the AFL (Australian Football League) asks, 'What are the nicknames for the Victorian Football League teams and what are their theme songs?' I have to phone my grandsons in Melbourne to find the answer to that one.

I meet Michèle Valencia, who has translated all of the

Bony books. These are detective novels written in the 1960s by Englishman Arthur Upfield and set in many of Australia's most unusual places. They are bestsellers in France because the French love *romans policiers* (detective stories) – there is even a special library in Paris for crime literature. The Bony books have beautiful covers portraying Australian Aboriginal art designs and they are inexpensive because they are produced as *livres poches* – pocket-books, much smaller in size than our paperbacks. (At the bookshop I have a difficult time explaining – or apologising – for the fact that we do not have these small, inexpensive pocket-book editions.)

When Michèle and I discuss the Bony books, which are about the adventures of an Aboriginal detective, I try to explain that they are not much read in Australia now because the language of the 1960s is outdated and is now considered by many to have racist connotations. She can't understand this, because, she says, when translated, the books are transformed into modern-day French which is not pejorative or racist while the settings remain as colourful and exotic as Upfield obviously intended.

Another of my customers is doing a *doctorat* on Upfield so I have ended up learning quite a lot about this author. One day, I am invited to speak about 'Australian books translated into French' to some high school students as well as to the friends of the local library at Avranches, a beautiful little town near Mont-Saint-Michel in Normandy. Avranches describes itself as the '*Cite des Manuscrits du Mont-Saint-Michel*' because the library has a huge collection of wonderful mediaeval manuscripts dating from the eighth to the fifteenth centuries. They were deposited at Avranches in 1791. I stay at the home of a charming high-school teacher who shows me a large map of Australia, with coloured pins on it marking the settings of all the Upfield books he has read. It is interesting to see that the markers are spread all around Australia, in what are now major tourist attractions. I wonder why someone hasn't organised a Bony tour of Australia, but realise that it would be very expensive as the settings range from the Gulf of Carpentaria, at the most northerly tip of Australia, to Albany, the most southerly town in Western Australia.

In France, crime books such as the Upfield series are sometimes referred to as *romans noirs, policiers* or *polars* and are widely-loved and respected as a genre. Hundreds are published every year. Interestingly even here in France, the Anglo-Saxon translations are the best-sellers – Mary Higgins Clark, Patricia Cornwell and P.D. James. They are closely followed by French best-sellers Fred Vargas and Jean-Christophe Grangé.

My first introduction to French crime books was on a winter visit to Paris in 1988. My son David had a jazz group called Crescent and they entered a *Jazz et Polar* competition which was part of the annual Festival Banlieues Bleues. I was very vague about the meaning of *polar* at that time but, at the first round of the competition, all was revealed. The jazz groups had been given a section from a detective story and they had to improvise music that would recreate the atmosphere of the written words.

Many English-to-French translations are published *en grand format* (that is, as large paperbacks rather than as *livres de poche*; in France you seldom see hardbacks in adult publications, except for *beaux livres* (art books). Australian writer Jennifer Rowe has at least five crime novels published here, all in large format with attractive covers. Her books, and those of Peter Corris, Susan Geason, and Gabrielle Lord, all sell well. One of my bookshop colleagues complains that there are so many crime novels published in France it is quite impossible to read them all and very difficult trying to find enough room for them on the *policier* shelves!

We notice that the translators and university lecturers usually speak to us in English because they enjoy practising their language skills but students and the general public communicate in French, even though they may be ordering Australian books in English. Even when I direct them to publishers' websites they often come back to the shop and ask me to do the ordering as the instructions are too complicated. Most Europeans prefer the personal transaction in their own language and of course they love to be able to see the books before buying them. This is obviously one of the main reasons for the popularity of the Australian Bookshop.

⁓⊚ ⊚⁓

Visiting novelists this year include David Malouf (*The Conversations at Curlow Creek*), Helen Garner (*True Stories*), Linda Jaivin (*Rock 'n' Roll Babes From Outer Space*), Nicholas Jose (*The Custodians*), Gail Jones (*Fetish Lives*), Beth Yahp (*Crocodile Fury*) and Bernard Cohen (*Tourism*). Children's authors Hazel Edwards and Mem Fox also contribute to the overview of Australian writing and the *rencontres* now seem to be an established part of the Parisian cultural calendar.

This year we have presented some of Australia's best poets and the first *Au bout du monde* (To the end of the world) series of *rencontres* ends, appropriately, with a reading and talk presented by Edmund Campion, current chairman of the Australia Council's Literature Fund. He reads from his book *A Place in the City*, and afterwards brings us up to date with the state of Australian writers and books at the end of 1997. I have become aware just how quickly one becomes out of touch with events in Australia when living on the other side of the world. We are often asked for Australian newspapers but it is too expensive to import them. They are available at the Embassy but only during

216

office hours, when most people are working. Few people here are conversant enough with the Internet to take advantage of on-line news articles, so we rely heavily upon the visiting writers for news. At this, our final *rencontre* for 1997, nobody could be better qualified than Ed Campion to fulfil this need. As usual, the conversation extends into a convivial evening meal and for me this evening becomes a celebration of a successful, productive year.

After over a year of trading, the bookshop seems to have acquired a life of its own and is being shaped by the people who are associated with it. It has been a year of surprises, mostly pleasant, and as I review the progress of the Australian Bookshop I am optimistic and confident that in 1998, with the approach of the 2000 Olympic Games in Sydney, there will be many opportunities to capitalise on the anticipated huge wave of interest in Australia and its culture and so to bring lots more Australian writers and books to Europe.

Chapter 14

A HOLD-UP AND A THREATENING LETTER

'That bookshop was like her – a bright light that lost and lonely writers gathered toward, with relief at first, and then with love.'

Venero Armanno

PARIS, 1998

It's January and bitterly cold – there's no snow but a fierce wind blows the cold into my face and the only way to avoid turning blue is to turn my collar up and cover my face with layers of scarves, earmuffs and balaclavas. I dream of sunshine on the bright blue of Sydney Harbour, with lots of little white sails bobbing on its sparkling waters and people sunbaking at Nielsen Park. The Quai des Grands Augustins is deserted. The trees have long since lost their leaves and, although I usually enjoy the shapes of the bare branches and the clearer views of Parisian architecture that winter brings, this day has a bleakness about it, perhaps because of the lack of people to give life to the backdrop of the city.

Sunday mornings are often quiet – people sleep late and for many Sunday lunch is a regular family affair. After *le déjeuner* Parisians can usually be seen strolling in a leisurely fashion, perhaps through the Luxembourg Gardens, or along the quais where they like to browse among the books displayed on the little wooden stalls of the *bouquinistes* lining each side of the Seine from Pont Neuf to the Quai de la Tourelle. Sometimes they come into the Australian Bookshop but Sundays, it seems, are not days for buying books – instead the customers like to chat and fossick (*feuilleter les livres*, which literally means to leaf through the books), pointing out strange and exotic things to their children and each other.

On this particular Sunday afternoon there is no one in sight and the little stalls of the *bouquinistes* are all closed, partly because of the icy weather but also because of the big winter sales at *les grands magasins* (department stores) such as Le Printemps and Galeries Lafayette on Boulevard Haussmann. One or two people pass the bookshop, shrouded in heavy overcoats, woolly hats pulled down over their ears and thick scarves wound round their necks and faces, so I'm not at all surprised when a lean young man enters the shop wearing a black woollen overcoat and a matching balaclava, which covers most of his face.

I've been tidying some bookshelves so am not in my usual place behind the counter. He walks past me, towards the back of the shop and just stands there, neither speaking nor looking at the books. I'm not perturbed because we have some strange visitors from time to time – bookshops often seem to attract the lonely and the lost. I don't mind that, because they're often interesting and *sympa*.

I'm not sure what the man in the balaclava wants, so I wait for him to speak. Perhaps he's shy. He just stands there, and the silence becomes eerie because there are no passers-by and there's no music playing. Eventually, I can't stand it any longer, so speak to him, '*Je peux vous aider?*' (Can I help you?)

Without a word, he pulls out a pistol, points it at me, throws a small cloth bag onto the counter and says, in French, 'Put the money in the bag!'

Without thinking, I reply in English, 'Indeed I will not.'

I turn my back on him and walk out of the shop onto the quai. He panics, runs wildly past me around the corner into rue Séguier and quickly disappears from view. I don't know whether he was shocked by my tone of voice, by the fact that I replied in English or because I walked away. The latter was, in retrospect, a foolish thing to do because he could have shot me in the back.

He's gone and I stand there, trembling all over. I can't find my voice to call for help or to say 'Stop, thief!', which wouldn't do much good anyway, because there's still no one in sight. I've often had dreams where I lose my voice when I'm in danger and this is exactly what happens. I stand in the street for ages, speechless, trembling and feeling alone and power-less to do anything. I am too shocked to feel the cold. Nobody comes, so finally I go back inside the shop and try to phone my son, David. He's not home so I leave a message and then just sit there, wishing and wishing for someone to come.

After what seems an eternity, but is probably only about half an hour, my wish is granted and Venny Armanno walks in. Venero Armanno is an Australian writer from Brisbane and he's staying in the Keesing Studio at the Cité Inter-nationale des Arts. I'm so relieved to see him that I burst into tears and am incoherent for a while. He is understanding and comforting and stays with me until David arrives.

When David hears the story he says, 'Oh, Mum, that was very brave of you!'

I have to tell him that it wasn't brave at all, that I acted impulsively, without thinking of the possible consequences. It was only afterwards, when I realised I could have been shot, that I felt fear.

Vincent, who has a little French bookshop further down the Quai, comes by and is horrified at what I have done. *'Jamais, jamais*! Never, never do that again. Keep only a small amount of money in the cash register and hand it over. Your life's worth more than a few francs,' he scolds.

This is common sense, I know, but I acted without thinking. Besides, my previous bookshop experiences hadn't included any training in How To Behave If You Are Held Up At Gunpoint.

I go round to the local police station and although they are sympathetic there's little they can do. 'There have been a number of similar robberies in the quartier, but the thief is well disguised and escapes quickly,' I am told.

It takes me a few days to see the funny side of my response in English, because the feeling of being helpless and afraid in a big city was unpleasant and unexpected. Just when I am beginning to feel 'almost French' I become a frightened stranger. Horrible! I am, at first, deeply offended when an acquaintance tells me that he and his colleagues rolled round the floor with laughter when they heard the story but later I see the humour of the situation and can only try to imagine what the thief must have thought when he heard my stern, 'Indeed I will not!'

$$\text{\small{\ca{}}}\quad\text{\small{\ca{}}}$$

Despite this rather frightening episode, by June things are going well and we've sold about 450,000 francs worth of books, so I expect to break even after the Christmas sales and maybe even make a small profit this year, which will be ahead of target.

I have the most wonderful helpers this year – John Emerson still comes in every Friday and Claire every Sunday. Raphaëlle Pomian comes whenever she can and Patricia Brien, recently arrived in Paris, offers her help. Patricia is a young Australian freelance journalist who is enthusiastically supportive of the Australian Bookshop and comes in whenever possible; she is at present organising international book-group discussions at the bookshop and we hold regular meetings that are attended by an interesting cross-section of people from different countries. Creating a forum for some kind of international dialogue was one of my major aspirations when I was planning the Australian Bookshop, so I'm delighted by this development.

Patricia's reading-groups are going well – members of the group take turns at leading the discussion and some of them have been outstanding. I attend but don't usually say much because I don't want them to think I'm 'in charge'. One evening a French member of the group adamantly asserts that Australian literature cannot possibly have any classics because the country is too young. The ensuing discussion is animated and goes on for some time. In the end I suggest that perhaps it all depends on what you mean by 'classics' – she is not convinced.

During this period I also meet two other Australians who immediately offer their support – Kirsty Elliott and Dianne Lanham. Both women are warm and friendly. Kirsty is only in Paris for a short time but we continue to correspond – it is people like her, back in Australia, whose support helps the bookshop to keep going. Dianne stays longer and she too becomes totally committed to the project. Letters from friends like these keep me in touch with the reality of Australia and confirm the importance of what I am doing. Sometimes Australia can seem like a dream from this distance, especially as it is constantly being analysed and interpreted by many of our customers. The Australian Bookshop is becoming well known both here in Europe and in Australia and the cheerful help offered by people like Dianne, Kirsty, Patricia, John and the French aficionados is uplifting and keeps up the momentum.

We have big plans for the next two years, and we intend to take part in the 1999 programme of the Olympic Arts Festival for Sydney 2000, which will be launched in September this year. Olympic arts organiser Andrea Stretton contacted me last March and she's very keen for the Australian Bookshop to participate; she mentioned that Australia now has a Memorandum of Understanding with the French Government. I submit an ambitious proposal, which will include a stand at the Paris *Salon du Livre* (Book Fair) as well as some special events and marketing. Australia had never before had a stand at the Paris Book Fair, so this will be a big step forward.

The proposal is accepted and, for the first time ever, the Australia France Foundation has promised the Australian Bookshop a grant to help with the events. I am really excited about this and sign the acceptance of the grant contract on 30 July, before flying to Australia for a month to visit my family and to attend to some health problems which I have been trying to ignore up until now. It's also a chance to see my father, who is now ninety-three and in poor health. So I close the bookshop – it's the long holidays in France and many shops are closed even though the city is always full of tourists in August.

Although I'm concerned about Dad, my surgery goes smoothly and I return to France invigorated. I can't wait to be back at the bookshop to prepare for the Olympic Arts

Festival and to make sure that our sales figures keep escalating as they have done in the first half of this year. Life is good and I feel very at home both in the Australian Bookshop and in Paris. The first two days back at the shop are busy and there is a buzz of excitement as lots of people come in to welcome me back. *La Rentrée* in Paris is always busy and exciting as schools, universities and many businesses re-open after *les grandes vacances* (the long holidays) and the important French literary prizes are announced.

Three days after arriving back in France, it is mid-morning and I am sitting at the computer preparing orders for books from Australia when Guy, the friendly postman, arrives. We chat for a while and he tells me the latest news of the quartier – he's been doing this delivery round for more than fifteen years so everyone knows him and, though always discreet, he is a mine of interesting information.

After he has gone I sort the pile of mail – there's the usual advertising material, a few bills, some publicity material from Australian publishers and one envelope from the Préfecture de Police (police department). At last, I think, they have responded to my annual request for an appointment to renew my *carte de séjour* and *carte de commerçant*. This will be the letter stating the time and day of my appointment at the Préfecture.

I open the envelope, ready to enter the appointment in my diary and am surprised to see that it is not the usual slip of paper but a long letter. It is signed by the *Préfet* (Chief of Police) and begins by telling me that the Australian Bookshop has lost three times its *capital social* (capital declared on the business certificate) so the Préfecture is invoking two laws of 1938 and 1939 pertaining to business permits for foreigners and therefore cannot authorise me to continue the business.

I am stunned and confused because the Chambre de Commerce has my complete dossier with all of my financial details and the person in charge of the dossier knows that I have sufficient funds to support the business for five years. I had been prepared to write 300,000 francs on the business application as my available capital but the representative from the Chambre de Commerce assured me that the minimum capital of 50,000 francs was *normal* for a small business. I was surprised because that amount would barely cover the opening stock and renovations but bowed to what I thought was his superior knowledge.

Now I read on and my stomach turns to jelly – the letter says that I must stop selling immediately or I will be prosecuted. It gets worse because the next paragraph says I must leave the country by 1 October or I will be arrested and escorted to the border. Arrested and escorted to the border! It's a bad dream. I can't believe it. By now I am trembling all over and can't read any further. My heart is beating frantically, I feel dizzy and can't think clearly. It's devastating and seems unfair because I have no debts, have paid my taxes regularly each month via the accountant and have sufficient funds to keep the Australian Bookshop going for at least another two years.

I am alone in the shop and what I have read makes me feel sick in the stomach and totally bewildered. I can't think straight – I keep seeing the stern and formal language saying I must leave the country in one month's time and all the talk of being arrested and accompanied to the border by police escort makes me feel like some kind of criminal. All I have between me and instant deportation is this piece of paper entitling me to stay for only one month more. Although I skim the rest of the document, I can't concentrate and keep returning to the words 'illegal', 'prosecuted', 'police arrest', 'escorted to the border' . . . I can't believe that I am being treated like this in a country I have grown to love as my second home.

The dossier I originally prepared in Australia contained evidence of my assets – there was a question asking how much funding I had available for the business and I had to prove that it really *was* available. This dossier was sent to the Police Department here so I am astonished that they haven't contacted me or the Chambre de Commerce to discuss these things before sending such a distressing letter. The problem may be that the *bilan* or balance sheet of every business in France is available on Minitel for all to see and anyone reading mine would see that the losses exceeded the *capital social* but would be unaware of my personal back-up funding.

I try to stay calm and finish reading the letter. It is full of legalese and I can barely understand it because my head is spinning and my knowledge of legal French is minimal, but the general message seems to be that even if I begin an appeal, the present decision will *not* be deferred and I have thirty days to pack up everything and leave France.

It is confronting to be faced with an unexpected crisis in a foreign language. My normal thought patterns and reactions don't operate. In moments of crisis, it seems, you automatically return to your mother tongue (as I did during the hold-up) and I recall the words of a French friend who is quite adamant that you can never completely belong to a culture other than the one you were reared in. I normally feel so at home and so comfortable in Paris that it is confronting to suddenly feel like an outsider, an alien, a displaced person.

After the hold-up David said my reaction was brave but it wasn't – it was just a reflex action. Today's trauma is too much and I feel defeated because I don't know how I can possibly be ready to leave the country by 1 October. I panic and immediately cancel Garry Disher's *rencontre* (the only cancellation out of more than seventy events in Paris) and notify the Olympic Games Committee that I will be unable to go ahead with our planned project as I will not be in Paris next year.

I don't know where to start or what to do so I try to contact the French Chamber of Commerce representative, whom I've known now for several years, but he is unavailable and I eventually discover that he has been transferred to a completely different government department. I phone my accountant (*expert-comptable*) who says he will provide me with a statement saying that I have no debts but, otherwise, there is little he can do. The next day David returns from the provinces and he begins to draft a letter of appeal, but a French friend calls in on the same day and says we must challenge the decision formally; she gives me the name of a barrister she says will prepare an appeal. When I phone him he sternly tells me that he will need 5000 francs up front. I give him the money and a copy of the letter and he says that he will send me an opinion as soon as possible to advise me about the procedure.

I put a sign in both windows saying, 'Closed until further notice'. The shop is closed and the front roller-door is down. I go from being surrounded by people all day to sitting alone in the shop, surrounded by my books, visited occasionally by friends who aren't working. I'm in a state of inertia and when people stop to read the notice on the door I can't muster the energy to run out onto the quai to tell them the sad story of what has happened to the Australian

Bookshop. I make an exception for two or three students whose faces I recognise, and they come inside and chat about their studies. David is recording this week and I don't want to worry him because Paris Combo is enjoying a huge success in both France and the USA, which means that he is very busy, so I sit alone and wonder what to do next.

Chapter 15

THE DREAM BECOMES A NIGHTMARE

'Les livres font les époques et les nations, commes les époques et les nations font les livres.'

'Books make eras and nations, just as eras and nations make books.'

Jean-Jacques Ampère

PARIS, 1998

The news spreads quickly and Professor Martine Piquet, an academic from the Sorbonne, phones me to say she has collected over a hundred signatures from lecturers at universities throughout France and these have been sent, with a petition protesting the closure of the Australian Bookshop, to the Ministre de l'Intérieur. She faxes me a copy of the petition, which asks for a re-examination of my dossier so that I can continue to run the Australian Bookshop *'avec une compétence et un dynamisme reconnus et appréciés de tous'*. I am overwhelmed by their support and their words of appreciation. I have been working so hard I haven't had time to stop and ask whether other people are aware of what I am doing or how effective they think it is.

The next day, a journalist phones to ask me what I'm going to do and whether she can write about the letter for the press. I say that I am still confused and ask her to wait until I have calmed down and received legal advice on how to deal with the matter. I tell her I will probably appeal but am uncertain how the appeal will affect the present decision and whether I will still have to leave the country at the end of the month. I ask her to defer the article until I know what I'm doing.

She chooses not to wait, and nor does she ask to see the letter. She files an article for Associated Press, saying: 'An Australian bookshop that doubles as a de facto tourism bureau is under threat of closure because its owner has fallen foul of French tax laws.'

This is quite untrue – the letter has nothing to do with taxes. It is from the Chief of Police and it concerns an immigration law. She then goes on to state that, 'French authorities have advised owner Elaine Lewis her visa and business permit will not be renewed because her business failed to produce enough income.'

This is partly correct so she must have somehow seen a copy of the letter, but at no time have I discussed with her how I viewed the financial situation. The tragedy of it for me is that most people simply read the first sentence and as it is filed on Associated Press it is picked up by a number of Australian newspapers. I am contacted by someone from outback Queensland who has read the news and thinks I am having 'taxation problems'.

The remainder of the AP article is accurate but unfortunately it's the headline or lead sentence that most people remember. I have regularly paid my taxes and, in fact, the French Government has a lot of my money because I have been paying about 4500 francs per month to cover such things as health and retirement. Our Government doesn't have a reciprocal arrangement with France so if I'm not in

France I won't be able to claim what in Australia we call
'superannuation' and the French call '*la Retraite*' (retirement). Italy, Switzerland, Germany and other countries
have these reciprocal arrangements but, for some reason,
France does not.

But through my devastation I notice that wonderful
things have begun to happen, and my spirits rise. My
favourite postman, Guy, heroically suggests he could marry
me if it would help me to stay in France! (I *think* he is
joking.) Dozens of Australian writers and officials write
letters and emails in support of the Australian Bookshop.
Many of them write directly to me, which is heartwarming;
some write to the French Embassy in Canberra and others
contact the Australian Embassy in Paris. French publishers,
translators, customers and the French university professors
mentioned above write letters of support which are sent
to French officials. M. Jean-Paul Delamotte writes to
M. Chirac because he went to school with him.

M. Bernard Granotier, a sociologist, writes to the
Directeur des Libertés Publiques, Ministère de l'Intérieur,
stressing the importance of the bookshop as a link in the bi-
lateral cultural relations between France and Australia. He
writes that the Australian Bookshop 'plays an important role
in Parisian cultural life'. 'Meetings with Australian writers,
friendly drinks, cultural events, conviviality, all this con-
tributes to mutual understanding between the two nations.

As thanks for her selfless and devoted work, Ms Elaine Lewis is asked to leave the country by 1st October at the latest.' This gentleman has attended a lot of the events held in the bookshop but I have never had a detailed conversation with him, so his letter is an unexpected surprise.

M. Jacques Rancourt writes to M. Jean-Guy Boin at the Centre National de Livre on behalf of the Franco-Anglais Festival of Poetry, stressing the importance of the work we have done together in linking Australian and French poets and facilitating translations. Similarly, Marc de Gouvenain of Actes Sud writes of 'the importance of the diffusion of Australian culture into France as demonstrated by the Australian Bookshop in its work with publishers, journalists, translators and writers'.

It is wonderful to read the messages of support from Australian writers and community leaders. Many of them send me copies of their letters and they make me feel that creating the Australian Bookshop was well worth the effort and that there is a definite need for an Australian cultural centre of some kind operating as part of the Paris community.

Playwright Justin Fleming often visits France and his play *Burnt Piano* is set in Paris. On 13 October he writes to the Australian Ambassador in Paris:

'I protest most vehemently the proposed closure of the Australian Bookshop and the expulsion of its owner, Elaine Lewis.

'As a writer who has spent considerable time in Paris at the Cité Internationale des Arts, I had many opportunities to observe the role served in Paris by this unique bookshop and its most courteous and hospitable occupant. More than a bookshop, it is a centre for gatherings to nurture Australian cultural relations with the French and with international visitors to Paris. Ms Lewis has invested the shop with her own indelible style, which draws crowds of people who otherwise would have no opportunity to explore Australia's literary heritage.

Ms Lewis has devoted all her time and energy to this bold and successful enterprise, and she deserves every ounce of encouragement and support that we can muster.

I urgently request your intervention in this astonishing executive interference which would see it all come to nothing.'

✶ ✶

I still have not been granted permission to stay in France, either formally or informally. French friends seem to think I should just stay on but if I follow the letter of the law I must leave by the end of the month.

In early September I receive a phone call from someone at the Australian Embassy asking for an appointment to see me at the shop. They tell me that many Australian writers have protested to the French Consulate in Australia and that

I should have all my papers with me when representatives from the Embassy come to interview me at the shop because they are prepared to take my case to the highest *échelon*. They will be accompanied by someone of 'very high rank' in the Police Department. The words 'our spy', are used. This all sounds very mysterious and I'm not sure from this conversation who from the Embassy is coming, so I phone David and ask him come to the meeting, just to give me some moral support. Fortunately he's not on tour, so he agrees to be there. I am hopeful that they will say I am allowed to stay on in France.

On the day nominated we are in the bookshop, eagerly waiting to hear what I hope will be good news. Three people arrive – two Australians and a third person who is introduced as some kind of 'colonel' in the Paris Préfecture de Police.

One of the Australians, a gentleman whom I've never met or heard of until today, begins by saying, 'Well, you're finished, you know!'

'Oh no I'm not! Why do you say that?' I am astonished by his claim.

'Because you have two bankruptcies behind you.'

Shocked and indignant, I tell him, 'I have never been bankrupt in my life and I don't intend ever to be bankrupt. Don't you think I would know if I was bankrupt? Who has said this?'

'The Finance Squad at the Préfecture de Police,' he replies.

'If the police are saying something about me which is untrue, then I will sue them.'

'You can't sue the police!'

'Of course I can! If a person or organisation is saying something about me which is untrue, I'm quite entitled to sue.'

'Oh . . .' he looks irritated by me. 'Don't do anything until I check with them again.'

With that, they all depart, without the usual formal French farewells. I'm not sure why the colonel was there because he didn't say a word and although I was able to defend myself during the meeting, I now feel emotionally exhausted and can barely think. I am confused and I don't understand the reasons behind this visit. David, as always, is calm and tells me not to worry as, in his experience, French bureaucracy can usually be negotiated and that's all that matters. This does not reassure me. The next day I receive a phone call from the Embassy to say that the police did *not* use the word 'bankrupt', so I let the extremely odd matter drop and authorise my lawyer to begin the appeal. He tells me in a dispassionate, gloomy voice that it will be a long, slow process.

Word of my predicament continues to spread and, on 9 October, Peter Thompson of ABC Radio National asks me to do a live interview for his morning programme. So here I am, sitting in the closed shop, talking to Australia. It's a strange feeling, but Thompson is an experienced interviewer and I feel comfortable talking with him. I tell him what has happened and that I've engaged a lawyer but am concerned because I've been told the appeal could take four to five months.

He asks me whether I think this is a typical example of 'French red tape'. I am torn because I don't want to prejudice my case, so instead of answering him directly, I explain that I knew when I started the Australian Bookshop that French bureaucracy could be very complicated and that I suppose I have to accept the laws of the country I'm living in.

I tell him I'm thrilled with the positive feedback I've received from both France and Australia but I don't know what they can do to change bureaucracy. We go on to talk in general about the activities of the Australian Bookshop and, although I'm still distressed at the thought of sitting here in this beautiful shop, surrounded by books I am not allowed to sell and still paying a very high rent, it feels good to be talking to listeners in Australia. A few days later, the Australian Embassy in Paris sends me a transcript of the interview with several words underlined – it seems they are pleased with it.

I later do an interview with SBS (the Australian multicultural broadcaster). Fortunately I don't have much time to think about it so am not too nervous about speaking in

French. It is reassuring and heart-warming to find that the Australian Bookshop is seen by these people to have been successful and important.

So much is happening that I'm beginning to feel as though I'm in the middle of a surreal dream (or is it a nightmare?) and it's impossible for me to calmly evaluate the situation. I am somewhat reassured when I receive a warm letter from Peter Shannon, the Chargé d'Affaires of the Australian Embassy in Paris, saying that 'the Embassy will do all within its power to support any review of your business status in France for the renewal of your *carte de commerçant*'. The letter refers to the Australian Bookshop as 'a focal point for Australian literature, culture, lifestyle and leisure not only in Paris but for all of continental Europe, offering invaluable assistance to teachers, students, travellers and the public at large'.

I become more courageous and go ahead with Shane Maloney's *rencontre* on 15 October. I dare not open the roller door so we all creep into the bookshop via the back door as though it's a clandestine meeting. I suppose this is silly, because there's no reason why I can't organise private soirées and if the authors themselves sell their books I cannot be held responsible, but I'm trying very hard to satisfy the authorities because I don't know whether or not the appeal will be successful.

People are still confused and I wish I could write an

explanation of 'the letter' and the whole episode for my Paris bookshop colleagues and the general public, because most of them only know what they can see on Minitel and think I should close down the Australian Bookshop – they are not aware that my business plan guaranteed funding for at least three years.

On the other hand, George Whitman from Shakespeare & Company comes to visit and says that he can't see what all the fuss is about. He tells me that he's had a number of disputes with French bureaucracy and has just sat them out. I tell him that he's more fortunate because he owns his property, whereas I'm paying a very high rent at the moment and I'm not allowed to sell books to earn the money to pay the rent. It would cost me a lot of money to squat here on the Quai des Grands Augustins!

Chapter 16

A REPRIEVE

'I was scheduled to give a reading at the Australian Bookstore in Paris, but by the time I arrived the police had already shut it down a day or so before. Elaine smuggled me in through a side door, showed me around, and then, as compensation, took me to a café on the Left Bank where we drank much red wine and she taught me how to pick up French men.'

Mandy Sayer

PARIS, LATE OCTOBER 1998

I'm still here, even though I have been given no reprieve.
The letters and petitions have not so far had any effect upon
French officials until, one day, after almost two months of
worrying and waiting, with no sales and still paying a very
high rent, a French publishing friend sends me a postcard
with the picture of the Chief Commissioner of Police (le
Préfet) pasted on it. Next to the picture she has written,
'Here's your man . . .'

After this things move quickly and a letter is written to
the Préfet, not by my friend but by someone who knows him
well. (The French have a name for this kind of intervention
– it's called *le piston*.) The day after the letter is sent, on
26 October, a man in uniform, riding a motorbike with the
French flag waving merrily from the handle-bars, delivers
a letter that says the Chief Commissioner of Police has
received the letter drawing his attention to my case and that
my request for the renewal of my papers has been given
provisional approval. As soon as I obtain a new passport
I will receive a new business card with the temporary
resident's card, renewable each year. (They have used my
maiden name only – usually both names are included on
French business documents – but I don't suppose it matters.)

I am astounded at how quickly things have happened – I had no idea who the Préfet was and even if I had known his name, I could not have contacted him. It seems like a miracle and I am very grateful for this unexpected intervention on my behalf.

As soon as I receive the news that I am permitted to stay on in France and conduct my business, I fax the barrister asking him to stop working on the appeal. He faxes back to say that once started the process cannot be stopped. I fax back a copy of the letter from the Préfet and resist the desire to say, 'Don't be ridiculous.'

I confer with a French lawyer who has volunteered her services because she is interested in Australia. She suggests that I send the barrister a registered letter from the Australian Bookshop, saying I estimate that he has done less than half the proposed work on the case, which should be worth no more than 2000 francs and that he therefore owes me 3000 francs. This brings results and I received a refund within two days. One of the things I have learnt in France is that any important letter should be sent '*recommandée avec accusation de reception*' (registered and requiring a signature of reception). This is probably good business practice in Australia too, but it wasn't necessary during my days in academia. My teaching experiences were relatively gentle compared to this bureaucratic tangle I am encountering here.

A representative from the Préfecture de Police phones to say that they have arranged a rendezvous for me on 2 November to restore my papers and this time I am invited to approach the building by the front entrance, which is always heavily guarded. Normally, to renew my *carte de séjour* I would queue with everyone else at the back entrance, opposite the Marché des Fleurs (the flower market) on the Île de la Cité and although we are all screened as we pass the entrance door it is quite informal. The idea of confronting the security guards alone is too much for me so, once again, I ask David to come along with me. I am glad he's here because we pass through two lots of security gates before being met by a charming woman, Madame G, who leads us up and down several staircases and along winding corridors until we are actually back on the other side of the building where I would normally have entered with *tout Paris*. There is another difference today – we don't have to queue and instead of going into a long bare room divided into little booths, we enter a very comfortable office which obviously belongs to someone more elevated than the army of *fonctionnaires* who deal with the daily problems of the *commerçants* of Paris.

Madame is very kind and the business is almost concluded when we come to the part where my new *carte de séjour* is to be pasted into my passport.

'I can't do this,' she says, 'because there's no room.'

Although the letter from the Chief of Police mentioned a 'new passport' I thought this one would suffice because it has two blank pages, so I say, 'There's room on the inside cover – it's the same as the other pages!'

'*Non, non*,' she says. 'This is not permitted'.

After a feeble attempt at trying to persuade her to use the inside cover page, we depart with our mission only partly accomplished. The next day I receive a new passport from the Australian Embassy and return to the Préfecture, via the 'tradesmen's entrance' this time, to have my *carte de séjour* formally reinstated.

Chapter 17

A DIFFICULT DECISION AND SAD GOODBYES

'Freedom is what you do with what's been done to you.'

Jean-Paul Sartre

PARIS, END OF 1998

I should feel happy and excited at the thought of beginning my life on the quai again but I'm not. While I am over-whelmed and delighted with the support I've received – it's a wonderful example of the power of the written word – in the end, it has been a long, lonely and stressful ten weeks, during which no books could be sold and the rent remained as high as ever. I feel enormously grateful to the French who have supported me but the general public and the expats here in Paris don't know the full story and some are behaving as though the life of the Australian Bookshop is over, despite the fact that my papers have been restored.

There is still a lot of tension in the air because most people don't know what has happened and still think I am in some kind of financial trouble. I don't have the oppor-tunity to speak out and explain what has happened. Apart from one phone call asking who helped me, I have not heard from the Embassy. I was unable to answer their ques-tions because I'm given to understand that the person who helped me wishes to remain anonymous. Jean-Paul seems to have disappeared and if it were not for the wonderful young helpers like Patricia and her friends, I would feel aban-doned. As things stand, I can't think clearly about my future. Despite the wonderfully affirming petitions and letters, I'm still devastated by what has occurred and by some people's reactions. During the past two months I've felt as though the ground has collapsed from under my feet and I've lost control over my life. I don't like this feeling and am fighting as hard as I can to overcome it.

I don't know what to do. I know I can't continue to pay the high rent for this prestigious and beautiful bookshop on the Quai des Grands Augustins. I know that the book trade is changing because Amazon.com has entered the scene and the French have finally begun cautiously to use the Internet. So I start thinking about renting a small bookshop with a much lower rent. This means that I must try to break the contract with the owner of 33 Quai des Grands Augustins, move all my books and look for a new address. The situation is much the same as it was in early 1996: daunting, but possible. Once again I must walk the streets, this time in search of a smaller shop.

In the meantime, I phone the owner and he agrees to allow me to break the *bail* (end the lease). We agree that I will vacate the premises by the end of November. It's heartbreaking and I can't help weeping at the thought of leaving what I have regarded as my main home in Paris. I love this shop and many of the people who have visited it have become friends. To leave it will feel like cutting off my right arm.

253

The French lawyer who helped me deal with the barrister approaches me and offers to help. She advises me to liquidate the old business and begin again. I can do a voluntary liquidation, she says, because I owe no money to anyone except myself. The same lawyer also finds me a 'nice little accountant' who will look after me. So I hand all of my papers over to him and he promises to take charge of my business affairs, including the voluntary liquidation, while I look for a new shop.

Yet another delightful young Australian woman, Jacqui Howard, who has just arrived in France, offers her services. She is trained in arts administration, has experience in organising Australian arts festivals and is exactly the kind of young woman who should be in charge of an Australian Cultural Centre in Europe, if and when we have one. She is about to enrol in an Arts Administration course at the Sorbonne. She tells me what a wonderful 'product' I have. I am not really thrilled at the idea of a bookshop being a 'product' but her enthusiasm is genuine so I accept her suggestions and, together, we begin to create a new business plan.

Jacqui soon learns something of French bureaucracy when, on her first day at the Sorbonne she is turned away due to a strike. She needed an entry card but couldn't get one until she actually went inside and saw her supervisor. There were guards on all the doors and they would not allow her to enter the building. This seems quite a typical French conundrum! Eventually common sense won the day and she managed to telephone her supervisor from the bookshop, but I will always remember her on that day, teary-eyed, saying, 'What will I do?' It seems we are all vulnerable in the face of unexpected complications, especially in a foreign country, no matter how much we love it and feel at home there.

With Jacqui's inspiration and experience, the new business plan is completed and we write to numerous Australian businesses who could be supposed to have an interest in the promotion of Australian culture in France to ask for sponsorship. We choose some businesses who have French connections and others who are known to support the arts. We write to all of the French towns who are 'twinned' (*jumelées*) with Australian towns and we also write to French libraries that may have an interest in Australia. The libraries turn out to have their own specific methods of purchasing books, which do not involve a small retail bookshop; the twin towns also have their own methods of obtaining books (these seem to be based on personal connections); and only one Australian business responds, via the Australian Embassy, with an offer of AU$3000 dollars per year, provided we display their plaque in a prominent position.

One day when Jacqui and I are busy sending letters to all and sundry, M. Vinarnic, the owner of the shop, pays us a visit. As always, he is immaculately dressed in an expensive suit and a beautiful woollen overcoat. He is as charming as ever but for an hour he expounds a conspiracy theory about why the bookshop was closed down, rambling on about 'enemies in the south of France' and the fact that I must have offended someone. He spoke of Josephine Baker and her many adopted children who, according to him, have important positions in the Parisian bureaucracy. He said that even if I resumed my business I would have a 'black mark' against me and would need to clear my name. He even spoke of the French Freemasonry. I *have* noticed the enormous number of books published on French Free-masonry but can't quite see how it is relevant to my position. When he leaves, Jacqui and I decide that it's not worthwhile to even try analysing his propositions. It is too preposterous; I can't really believe that not making enough profit is suffi-cient reason for having my name 'blackened', as he put it. We dismiss his visit and get on with our tasks.

Another rather surreal experience occurs when the cultural officer from the Australian Embassy arranges an interview for me with M. Jean-Guy Boin, of the Centre Nationale du Livre. When I reach the Centre, on rue de Verneuil, neither he nor I know exactly why we are meeting. He explains that if I were running a French bookshop he could help but that he has no power to help a foreign bookshop. The French Government is very supportive of small, specialist bookshops as they recognise their value to the community.

'Why doesn't your government help you?' he asks.

'Sadly, the government of Australia doesn't seem to understand the value of having Australian bookshops or centres of cultural exchange in Paris – or anywhere else, for that matter,' I say. 'One Victorian Member of Parliament *has* tried to help me this year but he hasn't been successful.'

M. Boin can only suggest I attend French bookshop training courses but these don't seem relevant at this stage as I have less than three weeks left to pack the books while contin-uing to run the Australian Bookshop, organise readings, work on the new business plan and look for a new shop. It's just as well Jacqui is here because I have very little energy at present and have to push myself to keep going even though, in my heart, I don't really know what will happen to the Australian Bookshop once I leave the Quai des Grands Augustins.

On 8 November, five days after the renewal of my papers and the re-opening of the bookshop, my daughter, Ginny, phones to tell me that Dad has died. Although Dad and I haven't always agreed in latter years, I am devastated and leave immediately for the funeral. The Australian Bookshop is again closed, with an apology and an explanation attached to the display windows.

During the long flight home I reflect on my father's life – he was a strong, powerful human being, with a great sense of history, and he was still living on his beloved farm at the age of ninety-three. I realise how much he influenced and shaped me, both as a small child and as a young woman. When finally I learned to stand alone, we had many differences of opinion which were often related to what I perceived as his insensitive attitude to women. But he was of his time and I am very aware of the good things he achieved in his life. I am especially proud of his deep love for the land he owned, which he expressed by planting thousands of trees and filling in the washaway creeks on the property. He has left his little corner of the world more beautiful than when he purchased it, which is not a bad epitaph.

Dad would have been pleased with his funeral, I think. The little church at Whittlesea is overflowing and people have to stand outside until finally the cortège moves off with a police escort. I think he would have appreciated the formal ceremony as he was a great reader and particularly loved to quote solemn and flowery stanzas from the grand Romantic English poets (counterbalanced by recitations of *The Man From Snowy River* and *Clancy of the Overflow*).

I can't stay very long in Australia because I have agreed in writing to move out of the shop by the end of November so, with not much time for grieving, I return to Paris to make plans to reform the business and to search for a new home for the Australian Bookshop. During my brief stay in Melbourne I register the Australian Bookshop as an Australian business because I have been advised that it might be possible to operate as an Australian business with an agency in France and this would perhaps be a more economical way to proceed.

The packing of the books and the move are traumatic. I love the quartier and 33 Quai des Grands Augustins has become my home. It's the end of a dream and I feel alone and disappointed. Jacqui has found a wonderful job promoting Les Arts Florissants, William Christie's famous Baroque Ensemble and, since the shop closed a second time I haven't had the heart to contact customers or to advertise another re-opening. It's just too late.

Claire is unable to help at the shop now because she has been promoted at the literary agency where she works – this means that she has a lot more responsibility and, as well, often has to read and report on two or three books at the weekend. John has gone back to Adelaide and I miss him very much. Jackie and Peter have also gone. Patricia still comes when she can but she has a lot more work of her own these days. Dianne comes to Paris once a year but she is not here at present. When she is here it's great because she is bright and efficient and speaks very good French. Some of the customers keep in touch. But this is Paris – people come and go.

Elizabeth, one of my first French customers, who has become a very dear friend, helps me with most of the packing, which goes on and on. Will we ever empty the shelves? Elizabeth begs for boxes from all kinds of businesses but, in the end, this is too time-consuming and I buy dozens of boxes from a storage facility. The shop looks as though a bomb has struck it.

A new friend from Western Australia volunteers to help and together the three of us pack thousands of books. I wonder how long it will be before I see them again. Without the help and support of these friends and other close friends who come in after work, I could never have coped with all the small details of this move. Each book has been chosen with care so it's like packing away a whole lot of old friends.

During this stressful period I receive support and practical help from unexpected French quarters – employees of France Télécom and La Poste. When I phone France Télécom to say that I am moving, an unknown voice says, in French, 'I know who you are. I've visited the Australian Bookshop. Don't worry – I'll arrange everything for you.'

The people at La Poste are just as kind and organise the necessary paperwork for my mail to be forwarded.

At the end of November the books are gone and the shop is empty but M. Vinarnic is gracious enough to allow me to use the premises until the end of the year in order to allow me more time to dispose of the fittings. Lionel's beautiful *pieds d'acier* (feet of steel) were custom-made for this shop and both they and the huge corrugated iron counter are much too large for the tiny bookshop I now envisage. His smaller offerings are already in a *gardemeuble* (storage facility) in the Marais. It's sad going each day to the empty shop but life goes on in a more subdued kind of way. The computer is at home so there's not a lot I can do in the shop, but I still continue to visit each day.

In the midst of all this, during November and December, I somehow manage to organise two *rencontres* – for poet Michael Brennan and novelist Victor Barker. They become the last two Australian writers to read at the bookshop on the quai. I am still working with the Franco-Anglais Festival of Poetry so during the month of December we arrange for Michael Brennan to represent Australia at a reading at the Sorbonne by sixteen international poets to launch the new edition of *La Traductière*, the bilingual poetry collection published each year by Jacques Rancourt for the festival.

After the last *rencontre* Victor Barker sends a message of support which I add to the folder of letters and posters recording the visits to the Australian Bookshop by Australian writers and artists. He writes: 'I thought that the Thursday night reading and literary gathering was excellent proof, if any were needed, that you fulfil an essential service in bringing together French and Australian readers and writers to further a better understanding of each other, and of each other's country, lifestyles and literature. I both enjoyed and felt honoured to be able to participate in the evening.'

I leaf through the folder and feel privileged to have presented so many Australian writers to the French public.

Soon after this, Lionel's beautiful shelves and larger fittings are removed and I close the roller door for the last time. So many people put so much love and energy into the creation of this space – it's a very sad farewell.

Chapter 18

THE VIRTUAL BOOKSHOP

'Elaine Lewis, a woman elegant, articulate and indefatigable, was of
that rare breed of bookseller who was also prodigious of spirit. She
believed her role to be literary in the broadest sense: encouraging
conversation and exchange, fostering aquaintance and curiosity,
offering support and advice to stray writers adrift in France. As one
of her stray writers I remember this most vividly: Elaine Lewis in a
cherry-red cape with matching cherry-red lipstick, sitting perched
on a stool in a dim smoky bar, listening with utterly indulgent
attentiveness to a young woman reading . . .'

Gail Jones

PARIS, 1999

Most of the remaining stock from the Australian Bookshop is in storage and the rest is in my apartment, together with the office machinery. Each night, from my bed in the corner of the room, I watch the blinking of the lights on the fax machine, the computer, the answering machine and gradually begin to feel that the Australian Bookshop is swallowing up my personal space. I start to walk the streets again, looking for a smaller shop. I feel sad and miss the old shop, the community around it and, of course, the daily visitors, many of whom I have come to regard as friends.

Suddenly my life has changed dramatically – I have gone from being surrounded by books and people, with all the responsibilities entailed in the day-to-day administration of a business, to plodding the streets and returning to a silent apartment each evening. One of life's greatest pleasures for me is engaging with other people and suddenly it has almost disappeared. Worse still, the Australian Bookshop on the quai has totally disappeared. It seems that all I have left of the dream is the virtual bookshop on the Internet, which at the moment is simply a way of keeping in touch with those customers who use the Net. I hope and pray that I can build it all up again one day in a less expensive shop.

Life around the virtual bookshop is unstructured and consequently I have the feeling that I am meandering along, getting nowhere. I continue to visit my friend Maria every Monday and she keeps me sane with her common-sense advice and interesting conversations. Early in the year she introduces me to an estate agent, Madame J, who is both practical and kind. It is she who finds me my peaceful little apartment in rue Monge, not far from the Arènes de Lutèce, which has attractive gardens, trees and benches on the terraces at the top of the remains of a Roman arena, destroyed in the third century. It was unearthed in 1869 when new streets were planned and diggings commenced. Long ago it was one of the biggest amphitheatres in Gaul and could hold 15,000 spectators. I have come to think of it as my front garden. On sunny days it's relaxing to sit on one of the benches, high above the ancient arena, watching with the passing parade of visitors – sometimes a huddle of elderly men earnestly playing *pétanque*, or a babbling *crèche* of toddlers riding tricycles, or perhaps just a squawking band of pigeons searching aggressively for scraps. If there are no visitors, it's a pleasant place to sit reading the papers and soaking up the sun because there are lots of magnificent old trees and the gardens are carefully tended, as are most of the public gardens in Paris. It's so much more peaceful than the little studio I rented in rue Etienne Marcel last year.

(2) PARIS — Les Arènes Romaines, rue Monge

I quickly feel at home in the 5th arrondissement, mainly because of Maria, Madame J and my *concierge*, Madame Bizot, who, unlike the 'dragon caretakers' portrayed on tourist postcards, is a small, gentle and self-effacing woman who takes her responsibilities very seriously and shows concern for the occupants of both buildings she looks after. Once again, I need a temporary business address until the voluntary liquidation is complete and the anticipated 'new' business is created. I can't believe my good luck when I discover a business very close to my apartment which offers exactly what I need. It is a well-established business centre offering business addresses and secretarial services. The owner is experienced, cheerful and efficient and becomes another important part of my life in this quartier. All of these Frenchwomen are warmly supportive and anxious to see the Australian Bookshop re-housed as soon as possible.

Although finding the new shop remains a priority, I am still trying to keep the business alive and visit my new accountant every six weeks or so to try to discover what he is doing. This is not easy because although here in France you are told that you need to employ an *expert-comptable* and you pay extra to have one, the work is, in fact, given to an assistant. I'm sure the accountant is meant to check the work but, in my case, his assistant seems to be making no progress and cannot tell me what is happening to my dossier. I focus on the hope that, as soon as the accountant has completed the voluntary liquidation and I have found the perfect shop, the Australian Bookshop will begin again with the main business nominally in Australia and a branch office in Paris but I *am* concerned because the voluntary liquidation process seems to be taking forever.

The positive side to being 'in the wilderness' is that I have more time to devote to both writers and the general public and I discover that the Australian Bookshop is still very much alive to many of its French devotees. In January I participate in a half-hour radio programme on Australian literature for radio station France Culture. The programme is called *Staccato* and the work involves preparatory meetings with journalists Claire Lienart and Stephane Martinez. I introduce them to Australian Bookshop customer Françoise Kral, who is currently preparing a thesis on Australian writer Mudrooroo, and together we record a segment which is used on *Staccato*.

At about the same time, French theatre producer Jack Vincey asks me to find copies of all of the plays and reviews of Australian playwright Karin Mainwaring. This takes some time but I manage to find everything he wants. The work is exciting because he tells me that director Muriel Mayette of the Comédie Française wants to produce Mainwaring's play *The Rain Dancers*. The Comédie Française rarely produces a non-French play, but Muriel Mayette, who is a shareholder, is fascinated with Mainwaring's work.

❧ ☙

Australian writers travelling in Europe continue to contact the Australian Bookshop so I begin searching for possible venues for Australian literary events. Paris has a long tradition of literary salons and cafés so in February Jean-Paul Delamotte contacts me and together we approach the Café Saint-Sulpice for permission to hold a *rencontre* in their upper room. Poet Peter Bakowski reads there and we all agree that it seems ideal. There's a good atmosphere and it is easy to find as it sits on the corner of the square, opposite the Eglise Saint-Sulpice, not far from the metro. Unfortunately our poetry reading seems to have been its swansong because, shortly afterwards, this old literary café, with all its memories, is taken over by a handbag shop.

Throughout the year we explore a variety of venues: Australian couple Deidre Gilfedder and Waddick Doyle offer their apartment on rue Mouffetarde for a *rencontre* featuring Nick Earls and Bernard Cohen. Deidre and Waddick are an Australian couple who have lived and taught in Paris for many years. I first met Deidre when she was teaching Australian Studies at the university of Clermont-Ferrand and I also met many of her students. Waddick teaches at the American University of Paris. Both are enthusiastic about promoting the arts. They are warm and welcoming hosts and the evening goes very well but I feel that it is a lot of trouble for private individuals to have their home invaded by fifty to sixty people, so decide to explore and perhaps extend the idea of the *café littéraire* – *rencontres* held in cafés, bars or pubs. Some interesting evenings follow with *rencontres* held at the Galway Irish Pub (Liam Davison and Amirah Inglis); Woolloomooloo Australian Restaurant (Robert Dessaix and Judy Horacek), the French-owned Bushwacker's Australian Bar (Nikki Gemmell, Gail Jones, Daniel Keene), a Canadian bar called The Moosehead (Alexis Wright, Linda Jaivin and Pluto Press publisher Tony Moore with Clinton Walker's book and film about Australian Aboriginal country music, *Buried Country*) and, finally, the mediaeval cellar of Carr's Restaurant (Andrew Riemer, Vanessa Bates, Chris Saunders and Patricia Page).

On the latter occasion, the cellar is packed and poet Arthur Spirou introduces the writers. At the end of the evening Andrea Stretton, who is also in town, gives a short commentary on contemporary Australian literature which, judging by the response afterwards, is warmly appreciated by both French- and English-speaking guests.

The spirit of the Australian Bookshop is kept alive through these gatherings and through emails, letters and phone-calls. One day the phone rings and I am asked to speak about Alexis Wright's book, *Plains of Promise*, on French radio. I agree to do so because I greatly admire the book and was impressed by Alexis Wright herself when she spoke at The Moosehead earlier this year. *Plains of Promise* is a powerful and disturbing novel inspired by the life of the author's grandmother.

The French interviewer introduces me as 'the most Parisian of Australians living in Paris' and, of course, I'm chuffed at that but during the interview I am asked general questions about Australian Indigenous communities and I decide that I have insufficient personal experience to be able to comment truthfully. I tell the interviewer that I've spent three weeks on Bathurst Island, but haven't visited any other communities. I'm worried because I feel that I don't have the right to speak on behalf of Australian Aboriginal people and that they wouldn't like me to do so. In any case, I was invited here to speak about *Plains of Promise*. The interviewer doesn't understand my reasoning and I leave the radio station feeling deflated and much more Australian than Parisian. The only consolation is that, when I arrive home, a French librarian calls to tell me that he heard the broadcast and thought I handled it well.

Not long after the radio interview, one of my brothers becomes very ill so I fly back to Melbourne to be with my family; he recovers but is unable to do very much. Sadly, we decide to sell my father's farm and I spend several weeks helping another brother sort out our parents' belongings. I don't think they ever threw anything away. They were married during the Depression and they never really forgot how it was in those days so they kept anything they thought might be useful – pieces of string, old newspapers, silver paper (I think they saved this for the war effort during World War II), tools – anything and everything. It's an emotional time as the photographs, letters and newspaper clippings tell the stories of their lives and those whose lives touched theirs.

My youngest brother has become the guardian of the things we can't bear to part with but it's horrible having to get rid of possessions that our parents valued – especially the books. I didn't think that I could ever throw away a book but there are so many that have been stored in outhouses on the farm and are in such bad condition that we eventually make the decision to take these to the paper mill. If I still lived in Australia I think I would keep them and take the time to look at them more carefully, with a view to restoring at least some of them. This just isn't possible so, with heavy hearts, we sort them as carefully as we can and take a utility-loadful down to the paper mill at Fairfield. We are distressed at having to do this because, like our father, we both love books.

Six weeks later, when I return to Paris, I phone a customer to apologise for not having responded to an order he had phoned in just before I left. I am sure that by now he will have ordered the book through another bookshop, especially as it's published in America and has nothing to do with Australia.

'No, I don't have the book,' he tells me. 'I would be very happy if you could find me a copy. It is for Catherine Deneuve, who wants to read from it for a radio programme she is making.'

I'm surprised, but quickly obtain the book for him.

One of the most exceptional Australian readings in Paris I have ever attended is organised this year for Linda Jaivin at the home of a Baroness she met on the plane to Paris. Neuilly is an elegant, leafy and wealthy suburb east of Paris, out towards the Bois de Boulogne, and Linda, her partner, Tim, and I travel out there together. We are not sure what to expect so I am there to sell the books on Linda's behalf, if necessary. The Baroness has told us that she already has the books at her home so I don't have to make the usual arrangements with the French publishers.

When we enter the lovely old mansion, we discover that our hostess has bought the books herself and is presenting them to each of the guests upon arrival – I have nothing to do except enjoy the party and all Linda has to do is sign the books. The Baroness introduces Linda enthusiastically and seems delighted to have discovered an Australian author. It's a wonderful example of gracious patronage and I find myself wishing I had enough money to do likewise. How simple it would be if I could just buy Australian books and give them away like this.

Chapter 19

THE LITTLE BLUE SHOP

'The Australian Bookshop was legendary long before I arrived in Paris. By the time I got there, it had just been reassembled in Elaine's apartment and I can remember standing among piles and piles of boxes of Australian books and thinking how lucky we were to have such a committed and feisty ambassador for our work. We need more of her, many more of her – we need people like Elaine everywhere there is a flicker of interest in reading.'

Nick Earls

PARIS, 1999

Madame J is sure she will find a new shop for me and, after several months, during which time we both look at a number of possibilities, she tells me that she has found a beautiful shop for lease, at the right price, just beside the Collège de France. As soon as I see it I fall in love with the little blue shop in the heart of the student area, a few doors up from Boulevard Saint-Germain – the position is wonderful and the shop is charming with its outlook onto the garden in front of the Collège. Although small, the ground floor has plenty of room for shelving and the basement could be used for *rencontres*, displays and storage.

Another few months go by while Madame J negotiates with the owners – the problem is that there are several of them and they never seem to be in one place at the same time. In the meantime, I continue the *rencontres* at irregular intervals, depending upon when Australian writers choose to visit Paris. In early September I organise two soirées in one week, which is no big deal, except that I have my first French hospital experience during the intervening three days. It proves quite unsettling and I feel very much alone.

To begin with, as soon as I have settled into my bed, a nurse arrives and asks, 'Where is your thermometer?'

'I don't own a thermometer,' I tell her. 'I've never owned one.'

She looks at me doubtfully and leaves the room, without taking my temperature.

There is another crisis when an administrator arrives to tell me that I haven't stated my next-of-kin on the application form. This is because I know that David is recording somewhere and won't be able to visit me and, of course, the rest of my family is in Australia. The hospital officials insist that they cannot go ahead with the operation until I contact my son and find a phone number at which he can be reached, if necessary. He doesn't have a mobile phone and by now he will have left home – I am not sure where he'll be. I know he's at a recording studio and, after some sleuthing, I find the number and the operation goes ahead.

I'm in a private room and nobody comes by during the night despite the fact that they insist I stay an extra night so that I will not be alone. At one stage I ring the bell and the nurse takes an hour to respond. She is very angry and tells me that she has much more important things to do on the other side of the hospital. My spirits are temporarily lifted the next evening when my friend Raphaëlle makes a huge effort to visit me at the end of a busy day.

I feel like an outsider (*dépaysé*) and the whole experience again causes me to reflect that it's much easier to deal with trauma or illness in your native language; perhaps we revert

277

to childhood, especially if or when we lose control of our bodies and minds under the anaesthetic. I suppose, on such occasions, it is more comforting and comfortable to be surrounded by the language of our childhood.

During this time I am dreaming about the little blue shop and the week after my operation Madame J phones to tell me that the owners have finally managed to arrange a meeting and have agreed to rent the shop to me at an affordable rent. I am jubilant as I have fallen in love with this shop and its setting. A new agreement has to be created and it takes several months for everyone to agree to the terms. This done, the agreement has to be drawn up by a lawyer – it's incredibly slow and I dare not tell anyone, just in case it falls through.

Jean-Paul Delamotte keeps asking me what I am doing but I can't answer him as nothing is certain until the contract is signed and the new business formed. I think he has tired of my vague responses because he has stopped attending the *rencontres*. We are not on the same wavelength, really, because we have very different aims.

At about the same time I am approached by several businesses with somewhat similar interests. They all suggest that we might work together but, in the end, none of them has sufficient financial backing for it to be feasible. This is a pity because I think I would have enjoyed collaborating with some of them. The Australian Bookshop's collaboration with

Arts d'Australie continues during this period and it is a pleasure working with Stéphane Jacob and various French and Belgian art galleries, who like to have a collection of relevant books accompanying exhibitions of Australian art.

෴ ෴

I am still anxiously awaiting news of the little blue shop when the Australian Bookshop is asked to take some books down to Toulouse for a European Association for Studies of Australia (EASA) conference. My relationship with the Australian Embassy in Paris enters the realms of the surreal once again when the Cultural Officer at the Embassy very kindly offers to have the books sent from Australia to Paris via the diplomatic bags. Australian publishers co-operate and when the books arrive I use a taxi to collect them from the Embassy. I can't lift the cartons of books but the taxi driver obligingly helps me. Life here would be easier if I had a van or a car but I don't have a garage and the thought of driving in Paris terrifies me.

I have a very pleasant meeting with the officials of the Australia-France Foundation at the Embassy and they agree to help with the transport of the books to Toulouse. A young Frenchwoman, who is working at the Embassy as part of her work experience, is enthusiastic and says she will be driving down to Toulouse and will be pleased to trans-port me and the books as well. I have paid for the books in advance, with no possibility of returns, so am thrilled that the venture is being supported so generously by the Australian Embassy and the Australia-France Foundation.

A week later, I am totally flabbergasted to receive a phone call from the work-experience student to say that there will be no help from the Australian Embassy and that the offer of transport is no longer available. No explanation is given and it seems strange that a work-experience person should be asked to make such a phone call. No doubt she is nervous and I remind myself that she is not speaking in her mother tongue, but her tone of voice and the language she uses are not acceptable – *la politesse* is distinctly lacking as she makes her pronouncements in a patronising and dictatorial way. Perhaps she has been told what to say but the rendering of the message is disastrous. I tell her that I don't appreciate being spoken to so disrespectfully and, although I realise it is not her decision, I express my anger and disappointment. This is a pity, as she is a charming and intelligent young woman and I would have preferred to continue the previous friendly relationship I had with her when she was a customer of the Australian Bookshop.

Somehow I manage, alone, to take forty-five kilograms of books to Toulouse via Air France while the Australian Embassy staff motor down. The books are pounced upon by the EASA delegates as most of them are relatively new releases and haven't been seen in Europe before this conference. There are several history books, some novels and a good selection of current books about Aboriginal culture. For me, this is a confirmation of the urgent need for up-to-date books for teachers of Australian studies in Europe. I feel vindicated but, given the circumstances, it is a tiring and stressful experience.

To add to my discomfort, a well-known Australian writer comes up to me and says, 'You call yourself an Australian bookshop and you don't even have my books?'

She walks away before I can explain that because I could only handle a limited number I had very carefully selected books relating to the list supplied to me of conference participants and their papers. I don't have her books because her name was not on the list. I suspect she was invited at the last moment to replace a keynote speaker who was unable to come.

One of the greatest pleasures of this conference is meeting some of the customers of the Australian Bookshop for the first time. We've spoken by phone and corresponded with each other so it's good to be able finally to match faces to names and to meet some of those lecturers who are so enthusiastically promoting Australian culture in their universities. Subjects taught range from Commonwealth Studies to Australian literature, politics, sociology and more.

Negotiations for the lease of the little blue shop seem to be moving along so a week before Christmas Day I say to Madame J, 'I'd like to spend Christmas with Belle's family in the country – is there anything else I can do to hasten the signing of the contract? It would be great to be able to celebrate Christmas with a light heart!'

'It's 99 per cent completed,' she assures me. 'The lawyer has almost finished the agreement and then you will only have to sign it. Enjoy a peaceful *réveillon*!'

Belle's parents, Robert and Françoise, and her brother Eric live in a beautiful old farmhouse in a *petit hameau* (a small cluster of houses with no shops – smaller than a village) not far from Bourges, the ancient capital of France. The area they live in is called Berry-Bouy and it is part of 'le Berry' in central France, well-known to readers of Alain Fournier's *Les grand meaulnes* (set around Sologne in the north) and also to readers of George Sand, whose favourite place was her house at Nohant.

The people of 'le Berry', sometimes referred to as *berri-chons*, have conserved many of their ancient traditions and are especially proud of their cuisine and local wines. Robert and Françoise are no exception and together they spend a long time preparing for Christmas – we know we are in for a treat.

The traditional *réveillon* (Christmas Eve dinner) at Berry-Bouy is as festive and generous as ever, with oysters, *foie-gras*, Robert's famous *pâté*, roast meats, salads, cheeses (including *le Petit Berrichon*, a special goat's milk cheese), desserts and fine local wines to accompany each course. Our hosts, Robert and Françoise, are welcoming and friendly and I meet their extended family and old friends. It's only a short break in the country but it's like being in another world.

On Boxing Day (which is not celebrated by the French) David, Belle and I return to Paris by train. Snow is falling and the city looks bleak and grey – it is cold and windy and the snow turns into sludge as it hits the ground. Because of the stormy weather, there are no taxis. The northern bus is waiting so I tell David and Belle to go. I stand in the snow for over half an hour waiting for my bus to rue Monge. It's a bleak homecoming.

The next day I am shocked to hear from Madame J that the deal has totally collapsed. The owners of the little blue shop are printers, whose main work is carried out in the *banlieue* (suburbs), and they have now decided to retain the Paris shop as a distributing depot. I am devastated and feel sadder than ever. Things seem to be going nowhere.

Chapter 20

MY PARIS UNDER WATER

'On the night of my 37th birthday Elaine was part of a small group of Australians and Parisians who took me to a secret little restaurant by a tributary of the Seine, where we ate *moules frites* and drank a little too much of the local wine. Later on this hot August night the river was looking inviting. Elaine was the first to strip to her underwear for a midnight swim. By moonlight she dived in. We followed, only later discovering the water was supposed to be full of diphtheria. We managed to survive.'

Venero Armanno

PARIS, NEW YEAR 2000

The twentieth century is nearly over and it's impossible not to be caught up in the millennium celebrations in Paris even though I don't feel like celebrating anything. I'm still disappointed at not being able to rent the little blue shop and, to add to my misery, for the past few months I've been suffering a debilitating pain in my left shoulder which turns everyday activities like dressing and cooking into slow, agonising events. Various specialists and several therapists have tried to diagnose the problem but so far nothing has helped.

All the same, I'm delighted when Australian expat writer Patricia Page invites me and three of my closest French friends to view the fireworks around the Eiffel Tower from the balcony of an apartment near Motte Piquet. Having once experienced the excitement and terror of New Year's Eve on the Champs Elysées I am pleased to accept Patsy's invitation to a 'box-seat' viewing, away from the crowd, which can sometimes become riotous after midnight.

Paris lends itself to *feu d'artifices* (fireworks displays) as it provides such a beautiful backdrop. With the Seine winding its way past the many flood-lit landmarks, it's a perfect setting for extravagant pyrotechnics. This year there is a great deal of media hype and the designer of this Paris millennium display says rather poetically that it will be 'a symphony of light'.

There is much anticipation, some of it caused by the electronic clock with the time displayed in large figures on the Eiffel Tower. It has been counting down for several weeks. We are watching from the balcony and, at the very last minute, someone on the radio says it is rumoured that the computers won't be able to start the display on time. However, it is only a rumour and, at the precise moment, the tower explodes into fire and light – though brief, it's a dazzling, beautifully organised spectacular. When it's over, the lights on the Eiffel Tower remain, glittering like diamonds, and a searchlight on the top of the tower sweeps across the city at regular intervals, perhaps a symbol of continuity and hope for the new millennium.

The week before Christmas there were fierce storms throughout France; ancient trees were uprooted, the Seine was the highest I have ever seen it and Paris was declared a disaster area. In some ways, the weather reflects my feelings at the beginning of this new century. Although the fireworks on New Year's Eve and the companionship of good friends are briefly uplifting, I'm not looking forward to the year 2000 because I haven't found a new shop and the accountant is taking forever to do the voluntary liquidation so that I'm still in a no man's land, unable to make any long-term plans for the Australian Bookshop, although I'm surprised and gratified at the number of people who contact my virtual bookshop.

I spend hours working on the computer. I was reasonably computer-literate when I worked in Sydney because I did my own layout using Pagemaker and Finale computer programmes. Now I am discovering how useful the Internet can be when searching for out-of-print and rare books. It's like a treasure hunt and very satisfying. When something goes wrong with the computer I am 'talked through' the restoration process in French so I'm extending my French vocabulary as well. Needless to say, I use a French keyboard but this can be a nuisance if I send an email using accents to Australia or the UK. At least I am keeping the business alive but can't wait to be in a real bookshop again.

The saddest thing that has happened recently is the death of my friend Maria, and, months later, I still have a profound feeling of loss. My Mondays with Maria were like calm oases in the rather turbulent life of the Australian Bookshop on the quai. She was a delight to be with and without her practical support and friendship my life here would have been much more difficult. She had an extensive knowledge of Paris and of Parisians, especially those connected with the publishing industry, so I always knew where to come if I needed sound advice. I stayed with her for a few weeks when I was between houses and she was wonderful company.

Maria had planned her own funeral and did not want any words, only music, so for an hour we sat in the little chapel at Père Lachaise and listened to beautiful music chosen by Maria and played by some of Paris' best musicians, her friends. A grand piano had been brought in and piano, cello and violin combined to pay homage to a long and full life. At the end, the violinist (her close friend Ivry Gitlis) stepped forward and played a Hebrew lullaby over her coffin. This image will stay in my mind forever.

Thanks to Maria, who introduced me to Madame J and was thus instrumental in my finding my apartment, I've been living in rue Monge for over a year now and feel at home in the 'village' around Métro Cardinal Lemoine. Despite making the effort to surface and host readings during this time, I still have the feeling of being submerged under water because of my lack of control over the winding up of the French business and my need to spend most of the day in the apartment, which is not well-lit and is now crowded with half the contents of the bookshop. Hardest of all to deal with are my continuing health problems. I try to get out each day and so I became very familiar with the area.

Almost in front of the apartment is the Collège de France garden at the corner of rue des Ecoles and rue Monge. It's always bright and well-cared for and reflects the changes of seasons with direct plantings and the lovely cherry blossoms which in spring line the corners of both streets. Beside the garden and over the road are the two bookshops belonging to the publishing company L'Harmattan; these bookshops have an immense store of books on Africa, the Indian Ocean, the Antilles, the Arab world, Asia, Spain, Portugal and Latin America. They boast that they can supply every book in print from those particular countries and regions and they have a huge stock, not all of it on display. I enjoy browsing there as it is full of surprises – I have discovered that Australia is included with Asia so that there are some interesting Australian books in their collection. L'Harmattan is also a publishing house and they publish numerous academic titles. One of their staff once told me that they publish one book on every day of the year. The Espace Harmattan, which is part of the bookshop nearest the college, hosts dozens of interesting readings, discussion groups and promotions.

I often rendezvous with students, visitors and former Australian Bookshop customers at the bistro on the corner, Le Petit Cardinal. This bistro takes lunch vouchers, so it's always busy between midday and two o'clock. Employees aren't allowed to eat in their workrooms so if there is no canteen available the employer is obliged to give them lunch vouchers (*ticket restaurant, chèque repas or cheques déjeuner*). This explains why there are always so many workers sitting down to three-course lunches in the middle of the day. Some of them save them up and try to use them for a special lunch or dinner. The employer pays half the cost of the voucher and the other half is taken out of the employee's wage.

When the bistro's not crowded it is pleasant to sit with a coffee or a glass of red wine, watching the passers-by. I particularly enjoy it if the sun is shining, because my apartment is on an inner courtyard so doesn't receive any direct sunlight. This didn't matter when I had the shop because the apartment is very quiet at night (except for a faint rumble in the distance when the metro begins each morning) but now that I'm home all day I have to go out to see the sun.

Walking up rue Cardinal Lemoine, past the house where Hemingway lived for a time, I reach the Place de la Contrescarpe, another good place for sitting in the sun and people watching. I also enjoy the walk from here to Mont Sainte Geneviève and the Panthéon, then back down the hill to rue des Ecoles and home again to my virtual bookshop.

Many of the Australian Bookshop customers now ask me to search for books which are out of print or difficult to find, so I look for these on the Web and write to contacts in Australia who have access to second-hand bookshops. I haven't advertised this facility, but 'word-of-mouth' seems to be working well, almost *too* well, as I'm often asked for books which have nothing to do with Australia. I can only conclude that because they came late to the Internet, French second-hand book shops don't yet offer this search facility, or perhaps they don't want to pay for the time spent surfing the Net. I know it's not cost-effective but I enjoy searching and it's always a thrill to find that elusive book! Up until now, it hasn't been so noticeable in France, but the *l'Internet* is certainly changing the book trade.

❧ ❧

The *rencontres* are now held at the Café de la Mairie – it becomes a haven for the friends of the Australian Bookshop (and for me). Australian writers visiting Paris can, if they wish, present their work in the upstairs room of this famous literary café which is still used by writers, editors and publishers. One day a young New Zealand writer insists on reading several chapters of his new book aloud to me in the *salle en haut*. I tell him that I'm not particularly qualified to judge his writing but he doesn't listen. Nobody seems to mind his reading aloud, so he goes ahead and I do my best to help him.

Not far from the Café de la Mairie, at Saint-Germain-des-Prés, there are two other famous literary cafes – Café Flore and the Café aux Deux Magots – which also evoke the era of writers such as Simone de Beauvoir, Jean-Paul Sartre, Ernest Hemingway, James Joyce and Janet Flanner, the *New Yorker* columnist whose bi-weekly letters vividly portray life in pre- and post-war Paris (between 1934 and 1964). I love her books because she writes in detail about the people, the politics, the culture – every facet of life in those exciting, turbulent and rapidly changing days.

Of these three literary cafés, I prefer the Café de la Mairie because it seems more authentic and has changed little, despite the visiting tourists who usually sit in rows in front of the café where they can watch the passers-by and look at the water playing on the fountain in front of the rather forbidding façade of the Saint-Sulpice church. The upstairs room at the Café de la Mairie has its own special atmosphere – cosy and warm in winter, but very hot in summer, when the windows overlooking the fountain in the square are flung open and you can see the light playing on the water and filtering through the lacy green canopies of the chestnut trees.

At the beginning of this year, when I was looking for a home for the *rencontres* I attended a French literary evening at the Café de la Mairie to try to gauge the atmosphere. I slithered in, trying to look inconspicuous, and sat in a corner near the windows. However I wasn't permitted to be anonymous because the *animateur* (master of ceremonies) welcomed me and asked me to introduce myself to the group. So much for anonymity! The waiters were friendly, obliging and professional, first making sure that each person bought a coffee or a drink of some kind and then closing the door, saying they would leave us in peace until we sent for them.

I've been to other literary cafés where the waiters continually interrupt and I find this is distracting, especially for the readers. One evening at the Café Flore, English writer A.S. Byatt was presenting her latest work when suddenly a waiter appeared and tried to catch her attention. She was obviously annoyed and indicated that he should leave. He persisted until finally she leaned over to hear what he had to say. She looked shocked and then announced to us all that Iris Murdoch had just died and the BBC wanted her to speak live to air. She said that as Iris Murdoch had been a role model for her she had to go downstairs immediately to take the phone call.

PARIS. — La Grande Crue de la Seine (janvier 1910).
Inondation de la Rue Saint-André-des-Arts. — ND Phot.

For the French, these literary cafés are part of *le patri-moine*, icons which are revered and of which they are justifiably proud. An author friend was teaching creative writing in English to a group of French students once, and arranged for them to read their work at the Café de la Mairie because she thought it might inspire them. One member of the class was so overcome at the idea that when the day of the reading arrived, he began drinking steadily to calm his nerves. By the time evening came he was quite unable to participate.

There are small literary soirées, poetry readings, *cafés philosophes* and cultural events held in Paris every night of the week and this is part of what makes Parisian life so stimulating. At most of them, you pay nothing or perhaps buy a coffee or a glass of mineral water, wine or *une bière*. It's not the same as it was between the two World Wars or even after World War II (how can it be?) but publishers, writers, booksellers and readers still meet in the upstairs room at the Café de la Mairie and on a hot summer's night with the windows open and the church bells pealing, time can stand still for a few hours.

Australian couple Jacqueline Dutton and Peter Barber offer their support this year – I'm unable to carry heavy loads and they are always there to help me provide books for the *rencontres* and to give moral support. Jackie is in Paris for research and Peter is accompanying her. The continuing existence of the Australian Bookshop, in all its guises, has been totally due to the energy and enthusiasm of its supporters. Friends like Raphaëlle, Diane, Elisabeth, Claire, Felicity and others give me the energy to keep going, as I feel I must, because I still believe strongly in the importance of giving Australian writers a voice in the international community.

⤬⤬⤬

In early February I accept Susan Ballyn's invitation to take some Australian books to Barcelona University's Australian Studies Conference, called 'Changing Geographies: Australia in the Millennium'. I am excited because Barcelona has a long association with Australian culture – twenty-six years ago the Department of English at the University of Barcelona introduced the study of Australian history and literature. In 1988 Professor Doirann MacDermott, then Professor of English Literature and Language at the University of Barcelona, said that Spanish students were often interested in Australia, partly because it is so remote for them that they only catch glimpses of it in the cinema or on TV. She also pointed out that there are comparisons between the landscapes of the two countries and their colonial histories. Today Professor Susan Ballyn is head of a thriving Australian Studies Centre, founded this year and made up of six areas of study: art, archives and documentation, philology and literature, natural history, anthropology, and health sciences. Dr Ballyn has been enormously influential in promoting Australian writers in Spain and we have worked together when possible, exchanging information about visiting writers.

I love Barcelona (after Paris, it's my favourite European city) so set out enthusiastically with a suitcase full of books. The case has wheels, so I manage it quite well until I arrive at the university hostel where I am horrified to see about thirty steps awaiting me. My shoulder is incredibly painful and I know I can't lift the suitcase so I wait and wait until finally a strong, young student arrives and comes to my rescue. On the day I leave the hostel I solve the problem by allowing the case to slide down the steps. I've recently had to do this in the Paris metro and it works well as long as the books are carefully packed. Needs must!

As in Toulouse, the European participants at this confer- ence are delighted to see Australian books. I had ordered a number of new books and, again, tried to follow the themes of the conference – they seem very happy about the choices available. It would be a step forward if suitable books could be made available at all overseas Australian studies confer- ences. A few enterprising publishers already send samples but they are only a handful, compared with what is needed.

I meet, for the first time, some of the Australian Bookshop's Spanish customers. I've built up some close friendships by email and am delighted when one of them rushes up to give me a big hug. On the last day, while most people are saying their farewells over a glass of wine, I'm packing up the books and am moved when another good Samaritan, Sylvia Lawson, appears to give me a hand.

I decide to try Expolangues 2000 as a venue for promoting Australian writers. Expolangues is an annual *salon* (fair) that takes place in February, and this year Australia is the guest of honour. Because the event is advertised as a fair to promote languages, culture and international exchange I think it should be an ideal place for Australian writers to meet the French public.

I have been notified by contacts that there are more than thirteen Australian writers in Europe this month so I invite them all to participate in a 'Meet the Writers' programme, which will be part of Australia's contribution to the festival. With the help of the Australia Council I organise accommodation and travel and liaise with Harriet O'Malley, the Australian Embassy's Cultural Officer, who kindly organises two display cupboards so that we can have Australian books on permanent display during the fair in the huge hall at La Villette.

Visiting writers include Frank Moorhouse, Nikki Gemmell, Gail Jones, Merrill Findlay, Nicholas Riemer, David Reiter, Peter Barber, Andrew Riemer and Julia Leigh. It is Julia Leigh's first visit to Paris and the Australian

Bookshop, with the help of the Australia Council, pays to bring her over from London. Marc de Gouvenain of Actes Sud comes to Expolangues, meets Julia and buys her book, *The Hunter.* Participating expat authors living in Paris at this time are Beth Yahp, Arthur Spyrou, Patricia Page and Tim Baker. Many of the writers are filmed for a television programme in New Caledonia so there is ongoing interest and publicity following Expolangues, including newspaper articles in Paris and Australia.

The negative side of this 'experiment' is that some of the people on the official Australian educational stand tell me that they don't really want visitors to come down to our 'cultural section' because they prefer them to stay on the main stand which is trying to sell Australian education in France. There are representatives of many Australian universities and educational institutions on the main stand and their priority is to compete with each other to obtain student enrolments. It is sad that they view us as competition but I can understand their point of view, which is why, in my acquittal report for the Australia Council, I comment that 'Meet the Writers' at Expolangues 2000 has been a worthwhile experiment, particularly because Australia was the guest country this year, but that it is not something to consider as a regular event.

At the same time as operating the virtual Australian Bookshop and organising events, I am trying to find a cure for the pain in my left shoulder which is so severe that it makes me cry out if I move unexpectedly. It's worse at night so my sleep is disturbed. I go to various specialists, physiotherapists and health workers over a period of nine months until finally I consult a surgeon at the Paris Clinique du Sport. He examines the X-rays and says, '*Oh! Les tendons sont totalement rupturés!*' (The tendons are completely torn.) He tells me that it should be operated upon immediately and that, under the Health Scheme, I will be able to go to a Maison de Repos in Brittany afterwards, to convalesce. The holiday in Brittany sounds wonderful but somehow I am dubious about the whole idea. The next day I meet some Melbourne friends who suggest that I return to Melbourne and have the operation done there. They recommend a top surgeon whose specialty is treating shoulder injuries and I decide to take their advice.

When I tell the French surgeon of my decision he says, 'I don't think anyone in Melbourne will be able to do that kind of micro-surgery.'

I assure him that they will, but he seems unconvinced.

Despite his misgivings, I return to Melbourne, the operation is successful and my shoulder recovers very quickly. The astonishing thing is that the tendons are *not* 'totally ruptured' – I had grown a spur on my clavicle and every time I tried to lift my arm the spur would cut the tendon. The Melbourne surgeon removes the spur with a tiny saw and I am left with only a very small scar on my upper arm. I feel like rushing back to Paris to show the surgeons at the Clinique du Sport and all the other specialists who have been treating me just what can be done in far-away Australia.

Back in Paris and feeling much more energetic, Madame J and I continue the search for a suitable shop as I work at maintaining the virtual Australian Bookshop and organising the *rencontres*. One of the best-attended events of the year is the bilingual *rencontre* with Robert Dessaix, presented by publishers Le Reflet and the Australian Bookshop at Woolloomooloo Restaurant on 6 April. The owners of Woolloomooloo are always generous with their support and this evening is no exception. It's a lively atmosphere and the soirée attracts an enthusiastic crowd of both French- and English-speaking guests. Robert Dessaix is an accomplished linguist and the French are delighted to be able to ask questions in French. It's always a great attraction when an Australian writer speaks some French because, even though more and more French people are reading Australian books in English, they seem to like discussing them in French. Also, I think the writer who speaks some French is able to form a closer and more personal contact with the French reader.

Another highlight is the Franco-Anglais Poetry Festival in May, when we again have a group of Australian poets to support this year's official guest, Peter Rose, who participates in the cross-translation workshops. At the two readings organised by the Australian Bookshop at the Café de la Mairie Australia is represented by Phillip Hammial, John Bennett, Nicholas Riemer, Peter Barber and Arthur Spyrou. If time had allowed, it would have been satisfying to translate all of these poets – cross-translations are a good way to begin international dialogue – but this time, we have to be content with hearing their poems in English only.

Most events (apart from the final concert) surrounding the Franco-Anglais Poetry Festival are small (twenty to forty guests), but the publicity is wide and they give the participants a role in the Paris literary scene. The French Government sponsors the festival so the invitees become part of the social and literary history of Paris as well as having their poems and translations published in *La Traductière*.

Size is not always the best criterion when gauging the impact of an artistic event. Many of the most exciting theatre and music performances I have heard in Paris and other cities were performed in the tiniest of venues. I think of some of the important jazz clubs and small theatres. When I read *Le Spectacle* or *L'Officiel*, with their programmes of the week's events in Paris, I am continually amazed at the range of entertainment available and the fact that many of the performances are held in small cafés, bars, pubs and spaces belonging to special-interest groups. The surfeit of artistic talent seen in unusual places is one of the greatest attractions of a longer stay in Paris and sometimes the serendipitous discovery of one of these events can become a treasured memory.

One day I receive an unexpected call from Madame Josette Rasle of the Societe Littéraire de La Poste et de France Telecom. I am surprised and impressed to hear of the existence of this group and delighted that they want to publish a special number of their magazine, *Missives*, devoted to Australian history, culture and literature. Of course I agree to help. The result is a well-edited collection of articles and it is particularly pleasing to see more than fifty pages devoted to Australian writing. There's also a comprehensive list of Australian books translated into French.

I can't help wondering whether Telstra or Australia Post would ever think of publishing a literary magazine. In French society the idea that the arts are a part of everyone's lives is taken for granted and one of the reasons I love being a tiny thread in this social fabric. I don't think I've ever met a French person who wasn't interested in cinema, music, theatre or books. During the lunch break, bookshops and music stores are crowded with people buying, reading or listening, and the most crowded section is often that of the *bandes dessinées* – the popular comic books that have become an art form in France and are eagerly devoured by young and old.

Another well-researched and highly successful Australian publication in Paris this year is the *dossier* (special report) *Australia, Australies: Littérature-Histoire-Arts*, featured in the magazine for booksellers, *Page des Libraires*. Judith Roze, the young Frenchwoman who co-ordinates it, tells me at our first meeting that she has very little knowledge of Australia. With the help of Australian and French writers she creates a comprehensive overview of its history, art and literature, including also a list of forty-eight Australian books translated into French.

When the report is completed Judith retains an interest in Australian books and we meet from time to time. Writer Beth Yahp is now living in Paris and she also helps with Judith's report, contributing an article on Elizabeth Jolley. Beginning with occasional meetings, we develop a semi-regular '*chouquettes* with Beth' rendezvous on Sundays at 11 am, in rue Montorgeuil, the atmospheric cobbled street behind Les Halles. Whoever arrives first queues at what is said to be the oldest bakery in Paris to buy a large bag of *chouquettes* – these are little *choux* pastry puffs sprinkled with coarse sugar that melt in your mouth when they are freshly cooked. We then meet at one of the little cafés and, when the weather's fine, sit on the *terrasse* enjoying our *chouquettes* with coffee. It's fun and we have lots of great conversations with all kinds of interesting people from many different countries, some of them Parisians and others just passing through.

⟿ ⟾

About halfway through the year, Madame J tells me about a little shop in rue Cardinal Lemoine, not far from the university at Jussieu. It's in a good position, the shop is attractive and, importantly, the advertised rent is affordable, so I authorise her to negotiate. Again, this takes forever because the members of the company who own the shop meet only once a month and they never seem to reach the renting of the shop on their agenda.

'Do you think they really want to rent it?' I ask Madame J. 'Obviously they are wealthy enough for it not to be very important.'

She replies that she's sure they *are* interested and, finally, at the following month's meeting, they agree to rent the shop to me. However, there is a catch – they have decided to raise the rent by a large amount. This seems immoral to me, because the shop has been advertised at the lower rate for months, but there is a law in France that allows the owner to raise the rent if the shop is going to be used for a different kind of business. In the past, this shop was used as a real-estate agency so they have the right to raise the rent.

I am so desperate to have a bricks and mortar shop that I am tempted to agree to paying the higher amount, but Madame J is outraged and strongly advises me not to do so.

I am bitterly disappointed and feel tired and without hope. After considering all the wasted time, the advent of Amazon.com and the fact that Europeans can now order directly from many of the Australian publishers and thus avoid customs and sales tax, it seems that my dream of a rejuvenated Australian Bookshop is going to disappear. I can't make up my mind what to do for the best and I still feel as though I'm swimming under water, waiting for the right time to surface again.

To make matters worse, various unknown sources in France and Australia start claiming that the Australian Bookshop no longer exists, despite the fact that I've registered it in Australia as an export business. It distresses me when I receive a phone call from a friend in Canberra who tells me someone there has announced to an assembled group that the Australian Bookshop no longer exists – it's a bit like reading your own obituary. I also read in a Paris paper that I have 'gone underground'. This is news to me. The story is being embroidered as the days go by. Although Paris has a large population, geographically it is really a very small city, so like-minded people are continually running into each other. This can be great and artists are very supportive of one another, but it does lead to lots of gossip.

I'm living in a no-man's land of indecision. I must decide whether or not to open a branch in Paris or to simply continue the virtual Australian Bookshop which I can run from anywhere in the world. Ideally I would like to have a home base in both Paris and Australia; to spend six months here and six months there. This would mean that the *rencontres* would be concentrated into a six-month period. But I can't make any decisions until the liquidation is completed and my health problems are solved and I don't think I can afford to maintain two homes, however small they may be.

For the first time in my life I am blind to the beauties of Paris. I feel so disappointed at losing the second shop that I trudge the pavements without registering what is going on around me. During the past twelve months I have put a lot of energy into maintaining the Australian Bookshop in Paris but am now finding it much more difficult to continue. I begin to wonder what the future holds for both me and the Australian Bookshop.

Chapter 21

A SUDDEN ENDING

'At evening drinks in Elaine Lewis' bookshop, I first met Aboriginal writer Herb Wharton, and later found someone who knew how Moorhouse was progressing his novel *Grand Days* in Geneva. This was our Algonquin, our Blumsberie, in Europe.

A francophile since schooldays, I have turned away because of two unpardonable events: the bombing by French assassins of unarmed peaceniks in Auckland harbour, and the closure by gendarmes of the Australian Bookshop. Ah, *chauvin. Tristesse.*'

John Bryson

PARIS, 2001

After months and months of waiting and attending numerous interminable business meetings, the expert accountant's assistant phones to say that she is ready to finalise the voluntary liquidation and has made an appointment at the Greffe du Tribunal (registry office of the commercial court) for early next week. She will phone me as soon as the liquidation is completed.

I wait as patiently as I can for the promised phone call but more than a week goes by and there is still no news. I phone to ask her what has happened.

'*Madame*, have you completed the liquidation?'

'*Non, madame*', she says. 'They sent me away because I didn't have all the necessary papers.'

This is unbelievable. After all this time she still hasn't succeeded in completing the task. She doesn't seem to know what she is supposed to do – it appears to be a case of the blind leading the blind.

I feel disappointed and angry. 'Just forget about it,' I say, 'I'll do it myself.'

I hang up and realise that I have no idea what to do. But I *do* know that I'm tired of their procrastinating and tired of not being in control my life so the next day I go alone to the

Greffe du Tribunal and simply tell them, in my very best French, what has happened and how upset I am that the accountant has not supplied the necessary documents after all this time. The official looks stern (they all look stern in this establishment) and tells me to wait while he investigates the dossier. He departs and I wait nervously for half an hour until he returns and says, without a smile, 'There you are. It's done. You don't need to do anything else.'

'*Merci, monsieur*,' I reply in an equally stern, serious voice.

As I pass the security guards on my way out I reflect on my long journey. It has been over four years since I was first so intimidated by these grand buildings with their long queues and their expressionless, obsessive public servants. Even today's *fonctionnaire*, who has been so unexpectedly helpful, was unable to smile and maintained his stern, humourless expression throughout the whole procedure.

At last I have learnt *système D*, which is French for getting things done in an unorthodox way. The term comes from the words *débrouiller* – 'to untangle' – and *débrouillard*, which means 'resourceful'. The French apply it to finding ways around all kinds of government regulations, including finding ways to pay less tax. I only wish I had mastered *système D* a bit sooner.

Now that the Australian Bookshop in Paris has been liquidated I believe that I'm free to either continue as I am with the virtual bookshop, registered as a business in

Australia, or I could investigate creating a bricks and mortar agency in Paris. I do some research and one of Paris' leading accountants tells me that I have been wrongly advised – in his opinion I should have simply 'put the business to sleep' for a while in which case it would have been much easier to start again. As things stand, it will be very difficult.

It takes a long time for me to decide what to do because I seem to have lost a lot of the energy and drive that has propelled me along for the past ten years. It's partly due to health problems, I know, but the thought of beginning again to battle with the bureaucracies of both countries seems too difficult and the French are increasingly now using the Internet to buy books.

I can't compete with on-line Australian bookshops and I can't bear to kill off the Australian Bookshop in Paris, which somehow seems to have developed a personality of its own and has become almost like a child to me. So, slowly and painfully, I make the decision to continue the Australian Bookshop as a small on-line business and to organise readings whenever I'm in Paris and the need arises. That there is a need for both *rencontres* and books is evident from the number of requests I have received during the period since leaving the Quai des Grands Augustins.

On a personal level, the ideal solution to my problems would be to live six months in Paris and six months in Melbourne each year. This is impossible so, very slowly, I come to accept the fact that I can live happily in Melbourne with frequent visits to Paris. I can continue to usefully promote Australian books in different ways – through the on-line Australian Bookshop, through the Franco-Anglais Poetry Festival and by facilitating events and continuing to build bridges between the writers, translators and publishers who are all part of what made the Australian Bookshop in Paris.

Chapter 22

A BIENTÔT, PARIS

'You must not pity me because my sixtieth year finds me still astonished. To be astonished is one of the surest ways of not growing old too quickly.'

Sidonie Gabrielle Colette

MELBOURNE, 2004

It is twenty years since our night at Opera Garnier and the Martha Graham experience. I am now in my seventieth year and the Australian Bookshop in Paris has evolved into a small on-line business that continues to facilitate links between Australian writers and Europeans interested in Australian books as well as searching for out-of-print Australian books.

The Australian Bookshop had a long gestation period but once launched it seemed to take on a life of its own. During the ten years of planning and dreaming, I never imagined the Australian Bookshop as anything other than a very quiet little bookshop in a corner of Paris. (Before leaving Australia I went to night school in Sydney to learn picture-framing so that I could do it in my spare time at the bookshop.) I certainly never dreamed that the bookshop would host more than seventy events for Australian artists and become such a well-accepted part of the Parisian community that hundreds of French would protest at its threatened closure.

That the Australian Bookshop developed its own identity was due to vast amounts of helpful input which often came from unexpected sources, starting with the

316

imaginative décor created by Parisian artists and including the hard work, energy and love of a multitude of volunteers and the thousands of customers and, of course, the writers themselves. The net spread much wider than I could ever have imagined.

The Australian Bookshop became a central meeting place for all kinds of people – not only for Australiana specialists but for writers, translators, publishers, home-sick Australians and tourists from all over the world. The small independent Australian book publishers, as well as the huge international publishing houses, at last had a place in central Paris where they could display their books and travellers finally found a quasi Australian tourism office, open until late on weekdays and all day Saturday and Sunday.

As for me, I have lived my dream and both the Australian Bookshop and the city of Paris will remain part of me. I now have a half-French grand-daughter and I am very happy to have experienced her culture. Whatever happens now, I will always be torn between the country of my birth and my adopted country – Paris is part of my heart and France is my other home. Material possessions have become less important so, like a nomad, I can move quickly from one part of the world to another.

It's partly due to the language but it seems to me that my French persona is different from the Australian 'me'. I love the language and even when I'm not there I still find myself thinking in French and using a French phrase because I can't think of an English equivalent. Sometimes my English is more formal than it used to be because of the influence of French grammar. 'What day are we today?' I sometimes say. Another interesting effect of continually speaking in French is that facial expressions change involuntarily because of the placement of the vowels. You only need to look in the mirror and say *'oui'* and 'yes' to see the difference in the shape of your mouth. Speaking French produces a sterner look than that of the average Australian, whose vowels are broader and attitude generally more relaxed.

When I go to Paris now, I always visit the Café de la Mairie as soon as possible and, *bien sûr*, if there is an Australian writer in town looking for a venue, I am pleased to assist. When the waiters say, '*Bonjour, madame*,' and I order my coffee, I feel as though I have never left and I haven't really, because, despite the fact that I now love my life in Australia, my Parisian life continually beckons.

Postlude

THE DREAM TRAVELLING-TRUNK

The dream travelling-trunk is gone. Abandoned in an outhouse and neglected by my tenants, it became so dilapidated that it was no longer worth keeping. I felt sad at first, but now it doesn't seem to matter much, because many of the dreams symbolised by my dream travelling-trunk have been lived. In my mind I now have two mother countries, and the big ocean liner, the streamers and the long farewells at Port Melbourne seem to belong to yet another life.

Appendix 1

PREFECTURE DE POLICE

DIRECTION DE LA POLICE GENERALE

le 1 septembre 1998

Madame,

Vous avez sollicité le renouvellement de votre carte de commerçant, en qualité de gérante de la S.A.R.L. «AUSTRALIAN BOOKSHOP» sise 1, rue Séguier à Paris 6ème.

Or, après examen attentif de votre dossier, il apparaît que la situation financière est très inférieure aux prévisions, et les pertes accumulées dépassent le triple du capital social.

Dans ces conditions, et conformément à l'article 1er du décret-loi du 12 novembre 1938 relatif à la carte d'identité de commerçant pour les étrangers et à l'article 4 du décret du 2 février 1939, j'ai le regret de vous faire connaître qu'il ne m'est pas possible de vous délivrer l'autorisation que vous sollicitez.

Vous voudrez donc bien, ne plus exercer d'activité commerciale, sous peine de vous exposer à des poursuites pour exercice illégal.

Le renouvellement d'une carte spéciale de commerçant vous ayant été refusé, il n'est pas possible de renouveler votre titre de séjour.

Il vous appartient en conséquence de prendre toutes dispositions utiles pour quitter le territoire français avant le **1 OCT. 1998**, sous peine de vous exposer aux poursuites prévues par l'article 19 de l'Ordonnance du 2 novembre 1945 modifiée relative aux conditions d'entrée et de séjour en France des étrangers.

Par ailleurs, une mesure administrative motivée de reconduite à la frontière par arrêté préfectoral pourra être prise en application de l'article 22 de l'Ordonnance de 1945 modifiée.

Si vous estimez contester la présente décision administrative motivée, vous avez la possibilité de former **UN RECOURS ADMINISTRATIF**

– soit **un recours gracieux** auprès du Préfet de Police – Direction de la Police Générale – 7/9, boulevard de Palais 75195 PARIS R.P. Votre demande doit être écrite, exposant vos arguments ou faits nouveaux et comprendre copie de l'avis de la décision contestée.

– soit **un recours hiérarchique,** auprès de Monsieur le Ministre des PME du Commerce et de l'Artisanat – Directeur du Commerce Intérieur – Tour Mattéi – 207, rue du Bercy 75 572 Paris Cedex 12. Ce recours hiérarchique doit également être écrit, exposer les arguments ou faits nouveaux, et comprendre copie de la décision contestée.

323

Le recours administratif ne suspend pas l'application de la présente décision. Il doit être formé impérativement dans le délai de deux mois de la date de notification de la présente décision.

Si la représentant du Ministre des Entreprises ou bien du Préfet de Police, ne vous a répondu dans le délai de **quatre mois** de la date de réception de votre recours, celui-ci doit être considéré comme **rejeté** (décision implicite de rejet).

***

*

Si vous entendez contester **LA LEGALITE** de la présente décision vous pouvez également former un **RECOURS devant la JURIDICTION ADMINIS-TRATIVE**, par un écrit, si possible dactylographié, qui expose votre argumentation juridique précise relative à ce non-respect de la légalité de la décision administrative. Ce recours juridictionnel qui n'a lui non plus **aucun effet suspensif sur l'application** de la décision donne lieu à un acquittement d'un droit de timbre de 100FF et doit enregistré au greffe du Tribunal Administratif de PARIS – 7 rue de Jouy 75181 PARIS CEDEX 4 – au plus tard, de manière impérative, avant l'expiration du 2ème mois de la date de notification de la présente décision (ou bien du 2ème mois de la date de la réponse négative à votre recours administratif).

Je vous prie d'agréer, Madame, l'expression de ma parfaite considération.

P. LE PREFET DE POLICE,

P. Le Sous-Directeur de la Police Générale,

P. Le Sous-Directeur de l'Administration des Etrangers,

L'Attaché d'Administration Principal

Ce document vaut titre de séjour d'un mois et visa de sortie. Il doit être remis lors du passage de la frontière au Service de la Police de l'Air et des Frontières, qui renverra à la Préfecture de Police après avoir mentionné la date de départ et apposé son cachet.

⤻⤺

Madame,

You have requested the renewal of your business permit as manager of the company with limited responsibility (S.A.R.L.), 'AUSTRALIAN BOOKSHOP', situated at 1, rue Séguier, Paris 6th.

Now, after careful examination of your dossier, it appears that the financial situation is much lower than the estimates, and the accumulated losses are three times higher than the capital funds.

Under these conditions and conforming to article 1 of the law enacted on 12th November 1938 relating to business identity cards for foreigners and to article 4 enacted on 2nd February 1939, I regret to advise you that we cannot give you the authorisation you request.

You will, therefore, no longer undertake a commercial activity, otherwise you risk being prosecuted for illegal activities.

The renewal of your special business card having been refused, it is no longer possible to renew your residency card.

As a consequence, it is your duty to make all necessary arrangements to leave French territory before **1 OCT. 1998**, otherwise you risk being prosecuted according to article 19 of the Decree of 2nd November 1945 modified in relation to the conditions of entry and residency in France for foreigners.

Moreover, an administrative step causing you to be accompanied to the border under police arrest could be taken by applying the modified article 22 of 1945.

If you consider disputing the present administrative decision in place, you have the possibility of using **AN ADMINISTRATIVE APPEAL**

– Either an **appeal for pardon** from the Chief of Police – General Police Administration – 7/9, boulevard de Palais 75195 PARIS R.P. Your request must be in writing, setting out your arguments with a new and comprehensive copy of the opinion regarding the contested decision.

– Or a **ministerial appeal** through the Minister for the PME of Commerce and Crafts – Director of Internal Commerce – Tour Mattéi 207 rue du Bercy 75572 Paris Cedex 12. This ministerial appeal must also be in writing, setting out any arguments or new facts, and should include a comprehensive copy of the contested decision.

The administrative appeal does not suspend application of the present decision. It is imperative that it is made no later than two months from the date of notification of the present decision.

If the representative of the Minister for Business or the Chief of Police has not replied to you within **four months** from the date of the reception of your appeal, this must be considered as a **rejection** (an implicit decision of rejection).

***

*

If you wish to contest the **LEGALITY** of the present decision you can also make an **APPEAL before the ADMINISTRATIVE COURT** in writing, preferably typed, which sets out your precise legal argument relative to the non-acceptance of the legality of this administrative decision. This legal appeal will **in no way prevent the application** of the decision taking place and a stamp fee of 100FF must be paid and be registered at the Commercial Court of PARIS – 7 rue de JOUY 75181 PARIS CEDEX 4 – strictly no later than the end of the second month after the date of the notification of the present decision (or the 2nd month from the date of the negative response to your administrative appeal).

I beg you to accept, Madame, the expression of my perfect consideration,

P. LE PREFET DE POLICE,
P. Le Sous-Directeur de la Police Générale,
P. Le Sous-Directeur de l'Administration des Etrangers,
L'Attaché d'Administration Principal

This document can be used as a permission to stay in France (*titre de séjour*) for one month and as a visa to exit the country (*visa de sortie*). When crossing the border it must be handed over to the Air and Borders Police (Service de la Police de l'Air et des Frontières) who will send it back to the Préfecture de Police after having written the date of departure and stamped it.

Appendix 2

LETTER FROM THE CHIEF OF POLICE
PROMISING THE RETURN OF MY PAPERS

This letter was sent by the Chief of Police (le Préfet) in response to a letter written to him by a very old friend of his, pleading on my behalf. The writer of the first letter was the boss of a friend of a friend of mine. In France this kind of intervention is known as *le piston*.

∝◦ ◦∝

Monsieur,

Par lettre du 30 octobre dernier, vous avez souhaité appeler mon attention sur Mme Elaine DRAPER qui solicitait la regularisation de sa situation administrative.

Il m'est agréable de vous faire connaître que l'intéressée a été mise en possession d'un récépissé provisoire, dans l'attente de l'établissement d'un nouveau passeport.

Dès qu'elle aura obtenu ce document, une nouvelle carte de commerçant, assortie d'une carte de séjour temporaire annuelle, lui sera delivrée.

En espérant avoir ainsi répondu à votre attente, je vous prie de croire, monsieur, à l'assurance de mes sentiments les meilleurs.

Cordialement,

Philippe MASSONI

330

∽◌֍◌ ◌֍◌∼

Sir,

In your letter of 30 October this year, you wished to draw my attention to Madame Elaine DRAPER who was requesting the regularisation of her business situation.

I am pleased to be able to advise you that this person has been granted provisory approval whilst waiting for a new passport to be issued.

As soon as she has obtained this document, a new business card, together with a temporary annual residency card, will be given to her.

Hoping this fulfils your request, I beg you to accept, sir, the assurance of my best wishes.

Cordially,

Philippe MASSONI

Appendix 3

ENTRIES FROM THE AUSTRALIAN BOOKSHOP DIARY

19 septembre 1996 Ouverture officielle de l'Australian Bookshop (Australian Ambassador in Paris – Alan Brown)
24 septembre 1996 Deuxième soirée de lancement (Mme. Sallyanne Atkinson – Austrade)
25 septembre 1996 Rencontre avec Gillian Bouras (lecture)
27 septembre 1996 Rencontre avec Herb Wharton (lecture)
10 octobre 1996 Un Pot Autour de Kevin Hart et Bernard Cohen
19 octobre 1996 Introducing Australian Poets: lecture de poèmes par William La Ganza
13 novembre 1996 Rencontre avec Thomas Shapcott (lecture)

14 janvier 1997 Rencontre avec Bernard Cohen (Vogel Prize Winner)
22 janvier 1997 Introduction à la littérature pour enfants australienne par Nicola Robinson
27 février 1997 Rencontre avec Fiona Capp – *Night Surfing* – and Steven Carroll – *Momoko* and *Remember Me, Jimmy James*
8 mars 1997 Rencontre avec Holly Kerr Forsyth
5 avril 1997 Recontre avec Raphaëlle Pomian et William La Ganza (lecture de nouvelles)

21 avril 1997 Inauguration de l'exposition photographique 'Dance Genius' de Angela Lynkushka

2 mai 1997 Rencontre avec David Malouf: lecture – *The Conversations at Curlow Creek*

8 mai 1997 Festival Franco-Anglais de Poésie, avec Gary Catalano (Aust.), Anne Portugal (Fr.), Maryline Desbiolles (Fr.), Luke Davies (Aust.), Vivian Smith (Aust.), Yves Bichet (Fr.), John Tranter (Aust.) et Claude Darbellay (Suisse)

15 mai 1997 Un Au Pot Autour de Beth Yahp

2 juin 1997 Rencontre avec Steve Bisley

5 juin 1997 Voyage en terre aborigène (art des Aborigènes d'Australie) avec Stéphane Jacob (Arts d'Australie)

18 juin 1997 Rencontre avec Susan Mitchell: lecture de 'Icons, Saints and Divas'

3 juillet 1997 Rencontre avec Hazel Edwards (livres d'enfants – *Hippopotamusing*)

24 juillet 1997 Rencontre avec Gail Jones (*Fetish Lives*), Gary Catalano (currently residing at the Cité des Arts) and Australian Poet Peter Bakowski

4 septembre 1997 Rencontre avec Helen Garner: lecture de *True Stories*

11 septembre 1997 Rencontre avec Linda Jaivin: lecture de *Rock 'n' Roll Babes from Outer Space* et Venero Armanno: lecture de *Strange Rain*

24 septembre 1997 Rencontre avec Nicholas Jose: lecture en anglais de *The Custodians* et en français (par Anne Rabin-ovich) de *Pour l'amour d'une rose noire*

9 octobre 1997 'Ecoutons l'Australie': rencontre avec le compositeur Peter Tahourdin, Elvira Kirkbride et Jacqui Howard

16 octobre 1997 *Smashed: Australian Drinking Stories* avec José Borghino, Tim Baker et Venero Armanno

23 octobre 1997 Rencontre avec Michael Edwards: présen-tation de *Perfume Legends: French Feminine Fragrances*

6 novembre 1997 Rencontre avec Fiona Capp: lecture en anglais et en français (par Marc de Gouvenain) de *Night Surfing* (*Surfer la nuit*)

5 décembre 1997 Rencontre avec Edmund Campion: lecture de *A Place in the City*

8 janvier 1998 Rencontre avec Dr Christopher Allen: présentation d'*Art in Australia*

22 janvier 1998 Rencontre avec Prof. Ken Dutton: *The Haunting of Dr McCuaig* by Kelver Hartley

29 janvier 1998 The Reading Group: *The Riders* by Tim Winton (author not present)

22 février 1998 Rencontre avec Mem Fox: lecture de *Possum Magic* et *Koala Lou*

3 mars 1998 Rencontre avec Judith Ryan – National Gallery of Victoria: Art Aborigène (in association with Arts d'Australie)

5 mars 1998 The Reading Group: *Strange Rain* by Venero
Armanno (author not present)
2 avril 1998 'Translating David Malouf' – David Malouf
and his French translator, Robert Pépin
8 avril 1998 The Reading Group: *My Place* by Sally Morgan
(author not present)
16 avril 1998 Un Pot Autour de James Bradley et Luke Davies
23 avril 1998 Rencontre avec John F. Williams: *Anzac
Myths and Legends*
5 mai 1998 Rencontre avec John Bryson: 'From book to film
– *Evil Angels*'
8 mai 1998 Festival Franco-Anglais de Poésie avec Tracy
Ryan (Aust.), Gérard Noiret (Fr.) et Kathleen Spivack (US)
4 juin 1998 Mike Dumbleton – Australian Children's Literature Workshop (International School)
7 juin 1998 The Reading Group: *Zigzag Street* by Nick
Earls (author not present)
18 juin 1998 'Images of Australia' – Herb Wharton (*Where
Ya Been Mate?*) et Martin Harrison (*The Kangaroo Farm*)
25 juin 1998 Launch by Jean-Paul Delamotte of *Rendezvous à Paris* by William La Ganza
29 juin – 10 juillet 1998 'Photographing Australia' – Lonely
Planet Exposition

8 juillet 1999 Rencontre for Liam Davison (winner of the
James Joyce Suspended Sentence Prize), Amirah Inglis

(resident at the Cité des Arts) and Australian expat writer Tim Baker at The Galway Irish Pub, Quai des Grands Augustins (a neighbour of the Australian Bookshop).

23 septembre 1999 'Andrew Riemer and Friends' – rencontre held in the cellar of Carr's Restaurant Cellar Bar. Andrew Riemer presided and was supported by Andrea Stretton and poet Arthur Spyrou. Guests writers Vanessa Bates, Barbara Brooks, Patricia Page and Chris Saunders. As part of the publicity campaign, the cover of Andrew Riemer's book, *Between the Fish and the Mudcake* was reproduced in the *Paris Free Voice* magazine.

31 septembre – 3 octobre The Australian Bookshop took 45 kilograms of books to the Toulouse EASA Conference and these were very well received, confirming the urgent need for up-to-date books by teachers of Australian studies in Europe.

18 novembre 1999 Un Pot Autour de Judy at Woolloomooloo Restaurant – Judy Horacek read from *Lost in Space* and delighted the audience with her straight-shooting comments on Australia today.

decembre 1999 Linda Jaivin. Launch of the French translation of *Eat Me, 'Mange-moi'*, at Woolloomooloo Restaurant.

13 janvier 2000 Nikki Gemmell in collaboration with translators (Dorothée Zumstein et Michèle Valencia) and publishers Les Editions Belfond et 10-18 (inédit) at Bushwacker's Australian Bar.

23–27 février 2000 Expolangues (18e Salon des Langues, des Cultures et des Echanges Internationaux) at La Villette – Australia was the guest country.

'Meet the Writers': the following authors were invited by the Australian Bookshop to participate in the fair with the support of the Australia Council: Peter Barber, Tim Baker, Merrill Findlay, Nikki Gemmell, Gail Jones, Julia Leigh, Frank Moorhouse, Patricia Page, David Reiter, Nicholas Riemer, Arthur Spyrou, Beth Yahp. The writers were introduced by Andrew Riemer.

Franco-Anglais Festival of Poetry

Since 1996 the Australian Bookshop has worked continuously with the Franco-Anglais Festival of Poetry, which each year invites an Australian poet to participate in the Festival, including three-day workshops with cross translations. Australian poets who have participated in this festival include Luke Davies (2005), Jan Owen (2004), Chris Andrews (2003, 2002), Sarah Day (2001), Peter Rose (2000), Peter A. Boyle (1999), Tracy Ryan (1998), Vivian Smith (1997), Andrew Taylor (1996), Kevin Hart (1995), Catherine Kenneally (1994), Pamela Brown (1993), Judith Rodriguez (1992), Thomas Shapcott (1989), Les A. Murray (1988), Alan Wearne (1987), Chris Wallace-Crabbe (1984).

The Association France–Nouvelle Zélande held two events at

the Australian Bookshop during 1997 and 1998 and the New Zealand Embassy bought two copies of every NZ book translated into French so that their French members of staff and visitors could become more familiar with New Zealand writing. The Paris script-writers' group Moving Parts met at the Australian Bookshop every second Sunday evening during 1998.

In 2000 the Australian Bookshop took books to the EASA conference at Barcelona and again, the warm reception of these books indicated the desperate need for a solution to the problem of quickly supplying new books to Europe.

6 avril 2000 Robert Dessaix – *Une mère et sa honte* translated by Ninette Boothroyd (Editions Le Reflet). Excellent presentation in French at Woolloomooloo Restaurant.

16 mars 2000 Playwright Daniel Keane and author Gail Jones read at Bushwacker's Bar and Restaurant

Avril–mai 2000 Article by E. Lewis in *Page des libraires* (booksellers' magazine) – 'Pourqoi je défends les auteurs australiens' (Why I promote Australian writers)

10 octobre 2000 Linda Jaivin – lancement et dédicace de *Les envahisseurs* à The Moosehead

17 octobre 2000 Alexis Wright at The Moosehead Canadian Bar and Restaurant, owned by Australian Michael Kennedy: *Les Plaines de l'espoir* trad. Sabine Porte

30 octobre 2000 'Buried Country – the Story of Aboriginal Country Music' video by Clinton Walker presented by Tony

Moore of Pluto Press held at The Moosehead Canadian Bar and Restaurant

15 novembre 2000 Beth Yahp, Tom Flood and Brian Castro (The Blue Mountains reunion) were very well received at the Café de la Mairie, Place Saint-Sulpice

29 novembre 2000 Barbara Brookes – *Eleanor Dark – A Writers' Life* (en anglais), Café de la Mairie

11 decembre 2000 Gretchen Miller's poetic sound picture *Text.Music.Sound – The Frenchman's Garden* delighted a packed room at the Café de la Mairie, Place Saint-Sulpice. Audio equipment supplied by David Lewis.

2001 Patti Miller – the Australian Bookshop held a rencontre for Patti Miller and also recommended *Writing for Life* to author/translator Christian Séruzier, who subsequently worked with Miller in France.

28 février 2001 Rencontre avec poète australienne Kathryn Gallagher at Café de la Mairie

14 mars 2001 Playwrights Karin Mainwaring and Justin Fleming wowed the packed room with their reading from Mainwaring's *The Rain Dancers* at the Café de la Mairie, Place Saint-Sulpice. *The Rain Dancers* (translated by Jean-Pierre Richard) will be premiered at Le Théâtre du Vieux Colombier – we celebrate an Australian first at the Comédie-Française

29 mars 2001 Angela Malone (*Lucia's Measure*) and Justin

Fleming (*Burnt Piano*) at the Café de la Mairie, Place Saint-Sulpice.

2 mai 2001 Visit to the Lycée Littré and l'Association des amis de la Bibliothèque – presentations in French of a brief history of Australian literature with examples of books translated into French.

17 mai 2001 Colloque bilingue avec Charlotte Wood (*Pieces of a Girl*) et Victor Barker (*Retours sur Tanger*, trad. Gabrielle Merchez)

19 avril 2001 Colloque bilingue avec Anne-Gabrielle Thomson (*John Higginson – speculateur-aventurier à l'assaut du Pacifique Nouvelle Calédonie/Nouvelles-Hebrides*)

21 mai 2001 Graeme Aitken – launch of *50 Façons de dire fabuleux* in collaboration with Editions Stock.

22 novembre 2001 'Le plaisir de traduire' avec Jan Owen (Australie), Jacques Rancourt (France/Quebec) et Anne Talvez (France)

2003 Beth Yahp – launch of French translation of *Crocodile Fury* in collaboration with Editions Stock – Café de la Mairie.

Acknowledgements

Special thanks to Jeanne Ryckmans – without her this book would not have been written. I will be forever grateful to her.

Special thanks also to Kirsty Elliott who supported me with patience and love both during the life of the Australian Bookshop and the writing of this book.

Thanks also to the Random House team – Nadine Davidoff, Jessica Dettmann, Peta Levett – and to my agent Jenny Darling for their warm professionalism.

To the Australia Council Literature Board of 1996 to 2000 – it was an honour and a pleasure to work with you all.

My heartfelt thanks to all the friends, helpers, writers, translators, publishers and teachers who gave life to the Australian Bookshop and a special thank-you to the readers, in Europe, Australia and elsewhere; I will never forget you.

And, *merci*, Paris.